Cuba at 25

Cuba at 25
the continuing revolution

by Gil Green

International Publishers, New York

Specified excerpts (verbatim and abridged) on pages 113 and
114 are from *The Fish is Red: The Story of the Secret War
Against Castro* p. 293 by Warren Hinckle and William W.
Turner; copyright ©1981 by Warren Hinckle and William
W. Turner, reprinted by permission of Harper & Row,
Publishers, Inc.

Library of Congress Cataloging in Publication Data

Green, Gil, 1906-
  Cuba at 25.

    1. Cuba—Economic conditions—1959- . 2. Cuba—
Social conditions—1959   . I. Title   II. Title:
Cuba at twenty-five.
HC152.5.G73   1984   972.91'064   83-22538
ISBN 0-7178-0608-1 (pbk.)

Contents

Cuba at 25

Introduction

We need to know all we can about Cuba—for our sake, her sake and the sake of peace.

Cuba is in the headlines. We are told it is a dangerous foe, a threat to our national security, a puppet state of the Soviet Union, and the "source" of the seething unrest and revolt in Central America.

A document of the National Security Council (*New York Times*, April 7, 1983), called for increased pressure against Cuba by a "quantum tightening of economic embargo" through enlisting other governments in this effort, by charging Cuba with human rights violations, and by stepping up U.S. military activities in the region.

Large-scale military maneuvers have already been held, some emanating from the U.S. naval base on Cuban soil at Guantánamo Bay, despite Cuba's insistent demands that the U.S. get out. Puerto Rico has been transformed into a huge U.S. strategic-military outpost in the Caribbean and Honduras is being similarly treated in Central America.

In a special address to Congress on the "Crisis in Central America" (April 27, 1983), Ronald Reagan accused Cuba and Nicaragua of building large armies for purposes of aggression and that this seriously affects "the security and well being of our own people." And a White House "Background Paper" (May 27, 1983) charged Cuba with being responsible for the "destabilization" of the region.

Replying to Reagan's congressional address, Senator Christopher Dodd of Connecticut, who has lived in Central America, rejected this explanation for the crisis in that region. "Most of the people there," Dodd said, "are appallingly poor. They can't afford to feed their families . . . they can't find a doctor for them when they're sick . . . they live in rural shacks with dirt floors or city slums without plumbing or clean water . . the very few live in isolated splendor, while the many suffer in shantytown squalor."

Senator Dodd said these are the real causes of the crisis. If Central America were not racked with poverty, hunger and injustice, "there would be no revolution." But instead of the U.S. doing something about these conditions, "this administration has turned to massive military buildup . . . and further military involvement."

In his address to Congress, Reagan had said that his administration "attempted a dialogue with the government of Nicaragua but it persists in its efforts to spread violence." Nicaragua's Foreign Minister, Miguel D'Escoto, told a press conference that this assertion was "nothing more than a lie. They've adopted a policy of systematically rejecting all dialogue with us."

Reagan made no claim for attempting dialogue with Cuba, for the U.S. Government does not even tender it diplomatic recognition. Such relations with Cuba were broken by Washington in 1961, the year of the aborted Bay of Pigs invasion. Thus today, after 25 years of existence, Cuba's Government is still unrecognized by the U.S., although Cuba does have diplomatic relations with nearly all governments of the world and with every other developed capitalist country. Yet when the democratically elected government of Salvador Allende was overthrown in Chile in 1973, the U.S. recognized the fascist dictatorship imposed by General Augusto Pinochet almost immediately.

On Cuba's part, it has advocated a peaceful, negotiated political settlement of the crisis in Central America. It has also favored dialogue and negotiation over issues of dispute between Cuba and the U.S. It would like to see renewed diplomatic ties with the United States. Only Washington's intransigence stands in the way. Cuba, however, will accept no other relationship than one based on mutual respect and equality.

Dialogue with Cuba is far from Reagan's mind. This can be seen by the unscrupulous nature of his speech in Miami, Florida (May 20, 1983). He accused the new Cuba of destroying "the strong

independent labor movement which existed before 1959," when the
only legal labor movement then existing was under the thumb of
Cuba's brutal dictator, Fulgencio Batista. Reagan also accused the
Cuban Government of suppressing the church, forcing young
Cubans into military service in foreign lands, profiteering from the
drug trade, turning Cuba into "one of the most economically
backward in the region," and that Cuba's Government was "a new
fascist regime."

In the course of this book we shall give evidence of the situation
in Cuba as we found it. At this point, however, let us merely note
how Cuba's daily newspaper *Granma* dealt with the charge of
fascism. It said: "If we were fascists, relations between Cuba and Mr.
Reagan would be excellent, as are his relations with all corrupted,
bloody and reactionary regimes."

WHAT IS BEHIND this villification of Cuba? Does anyone really
believe that small, underdeveloped Cuba, with only 1/80th the land
mass and 1/24th the population of the United States, is a threat to
us? It is true that the Bible tells of little David slaying the giant
Goliath with a simple slingshot. But the Goliath that is U.S.
imperialism is the most powerful militarist force in the world with
tens of thousands of nuclear weapons.

Cuba's arms are meant for only one thing—to defend Cuban soil
so tenaciously that the cost of trying to occupy and overrun it would
be astronomical.

What is really involved in the defamation of Cuba is the attempt
to lay down a smokescreen of falsehood behind which U.S. military
action can, if decided upon, take place. If, as Reagan charges, Cuba
is the "source" of the upheaval in Central America and the Caribbean, then, by this tortured logic, something should be done about
it.

That "doing something about Cuba" is on the Reagan agenda,
can be seen by more than the President's speeches. In April 1982, the
Administration, under the provisions of the Trading With the
Enemy Act, decreed that U.S. citizens no longer had a right to visit
Cuba as tourists. Americans could no longer see that country for
themselves.

Even though the Reagan edict against visiting Cuba was upset by
a federal court ruling in early 1983, the Reagan administration

appealed this decision to the Supreme Court, thus indicating its determination to prevent normal relations with Cuba even in so limited an area as tourism.

The reason given for continuing this denial of our right to travel to Cuba is to prevent U.S. tourist dollars from reaching Cuba. But two other objectives are most likely also involved: to prevent the truth about Cuba from reaching the U.S. public, and that there be few if any U.S. citizens in Cuba should Washington decide on military action.

In some ways even more ominous was the adoption by the U.S. Senate on August 11, 1982 of a resolution amending a budgetary bill, H.R. 6863. Introduced by Senator Steven Symms of Idaho, this resolution empowered the government "to prevent by whatever means may be necessary, including the use of arms, the Marxist-Leninist regime in Cuba from extending by force or the threat of force its aggressive or subversive activities to any part of the hemisphere."

The Symms resolution was adopted by a vote of 68 to 28. While it was turned down in the House of Representatives by voice vote, the Senate debate on it is very revealing. Senator Symms made clear that his resolution had Administration support. He quoted from a statement of Stephen Bosworth, Deputy Assistant Secretary of State: "The Administration finds this resolution is consistent with our policy, we support it."

Senator Charles Percy of Illinois, however, demurred. He tried to soften the resolution somewhat by removing the phrase "including the use of arms." He warned that the Symms resolution "might be considered a Gulf of Tonkin resolution for Cuba." (This seemingly innocuous resolution was passed by Congress in August 1964. It gave President Lyndon Johnson the legal pretext for all-out intervention in Vietnam. This was the essential purpose of the Tonkin Gulf resolution, although hidden from the public at the time of its introduction and passage.)

In the course of the Senate debate, Percy declared that the language of the Symms resolution could be interpreted "as an authorization for the use of U.S. Armed Forces against Cuba." Later he asked, "Is this the way we are going to threaten and rattle our sabres, and what are we going to do . . . urge war on Cuba? . . . What do we intend to do—invade?"

In a colloquy between Senator Dale Bumpers of Arkansas and Symms, the real intent of the resolution became clear. Bumpers asked Symms: "Does the Senator consider this to be authority for the President to take any overt military action?"

Symms replied: "I would say to my good friend from Arkansas that it is."

That so dangerous a resolution could receive majority support in the U.S. Senate by such a wide margin is a danger signal of how far things have gone toward military action. Nor is it accidental that Sen. Barry Goldwater followed up Reagan's inflammatory Miami speech with a public statement favoring a military invasion of the island with the objective of annexing Cuba as the 51st state.

We therefore had best know more about Cuba if we are not to be tricked and dragged into another military disaster.

WE NEED TO know more about Cuba for still another reason. Cuba is a poor, small, developing island, while the U.S.A. is a mighty industrial and world power. U.S. resources are incomparably greater than Cuba's. Yet in important human respects, Cuba is far more developed than we. No one there is rich and few own autos, but missing also is the appalling, degrading poverty so widespread in the United States.

Cubans also affirm that there is no racial discrimination, and that any attempts to renew it would be sternly punished by law. They also say that there is no unemployment in Cuba, that no child goes hungry, homeless or barefoot. Education is totally free, as is health, medical and hospital care. Cuban social services are generally admitted to be among the very best in the world. And, every working person in Cuba is entitled to a full month's vacation with pay each year.

Not bad for an "underdeveloped" country!

I HAD VISITED Cuba twice before; in 1969 and in 1970. Its revolution then was in transition from infancy to puberty. Now, it was approaching its 25th birthday. What was Cuba like at age 25? What changes had occurred since my last visit? How was Cuba doing? I had followed Cuban events from afar, but the urge to see Cuba again was overwhelming.

When I first visited Cuba in the spring of 1969, I crisscrossed the

island and met people in homes, factories, farms, hospitals and
schools. My impressions appeared in a paperback, *Revolution—
Cuban Style*. Now I sought to update that knowledge and to share it
once again.

I knew that a constitution had been adopted and a new electoral,
parliamentary and judicial system established. I also knew that
important changes had taken place in Cuba's economy, but did not
know how much truth there was in a U.S. Government document
that claimed Cuba's economy was in grave trouble. I also knew that
a Family Code had been adopted and a struggle begun for women's
full equality. I had read that peasants were now merging their
privately-owned farms into farm cooperatives, but I did not know
whether coercion played a part in this change. I also wanted to
know the reasons for the large exodus from Mariel in the summer of
1980. And most important of all, I wanted to learn first hand what
the Revolution, at age 25, meant now to the people of Cuba.

To receive help in getting answers to these and other questions, I
wrote a letter to Carlos Rafael Rodríguez, an old friend whom I had
known from years prior to the revolution when he was a top leader
of the former communist party known as the Popular Socialist
Party. He is now a prominent Cuban leader and a Vice President of
the Republic. He urged me to come.

I then wrote a memorandum indicating how I wished to update
my previous book to encompass the many changes since then, but
"without covering up or hiding problems that still exist—those
stemming from the past as well as new problems arising from the
vast transformations themselves." I stated a particular interest in
the democratic process and the problem of bureaucracy.

Thus, at the end of 1982, my wife Helen and I were on our way to
Cuba again. She would actively help me. We would compare notes
on places visited, people seen and interviews held.

1. Cuba again

All seats were occupied as the Air Florida charter flight took off from Miami International Airport. It was 10:30 p.m. and we would be landing in Havana within an hour. The other passengers all appeared to be Cubans—either returning home or visiting relatives. (The U.S. ban against travel to Cuba does not include family visits.) We had seen them lug oversized, bulging suitcases and duffle bags filled (we were certain) with goods reportedly scarce in Cuba. It was an animated, good-natured, Spanish-speaking crowd, obviously moved at the prospect of soon touching Cuban soil again.

Lost in my own thoughts about the weeks ahead, I found it difficult to reconcile the brevity of the flight with the enormity of the distance separating our two governments and social systems. It was as if we were being propelled into outer space, to be landed on a far-off, tiny planet in an entirely different universe. Before my flight of fancy was over, we were back on earth, in Cuba!

Havana's airport had not changed visibly since we were last there in 1970. In contrast to the sprawling Miami airport and its gawdy display of wares, it was indeed small and modest. Two other international flights had arrived at about the same time as ours, making the airport building even more crowded. At the same time, on the outside, hundreds of Cubans awaited arriving relatives and friends.

We had wondered whether we would be met at the airport so late at night, but as we stood in line to have our passports and visas validated, a tall, brown-haired, good-looking young man in his later thirties spotted us without difficulty. With Fernando García was a strikingly attractive younger black woman, Nancy Echevarría. She was to be our interpreter.

Fernando spoke English well; Nancy, to perfection. I assumed she had originally come from the States or had lived there for many years. But she had never left Cuba. A bit later, while waiting for the carousel to turn up our bags, we were introduced to Leonardo Consuegra. He was to be our driver. Shorter, stockier and darker than Fernando, Leonardo had a winning smile, proved to be a careful driver, a good companion, and was particularly solicitous of Helen. We got to know the three of them well.

We also became good friends with Fernando's wife, Olga. She had been asked to help organize our stay. Olga was indispensable, cutting through protocol and red tape to get us interviews with extremely busy people. But I've run ahead of my story.

As we waited for the carousel to make up its mind, and with midnight behind us, Fernando observed, "It's too bad that the first and last impression visitors get of Cuba is of the inefficiency of our airport."

"Don't worry," I assured him, "most people who come here realize that Cuba's resources are limited and that more essential needs must come first." Yet to myself I admitted that less sympathetic visitors might not react in the same way.

It was 1:00 a.m. before we were on our way to the Marazul Hotel, just east of Havana. We would stay here for the next three days, to relax and to digest the large bundle of "documentary food" that Fernando had brought with him in response to the request in our memorandum for background material in either English or Spanish. Fernando told us that Olga would visit us the next day. She would plan our schedule with us and then report back on progress made.

Our visit had begun.

THE MARAZUL IS LOCATED at Santa María del Mar, a short bus ride from Havana and faces the beach, north toward the Florida Straits, with the Gulf of Mexico to the West. Built since the revolution and designed by Cuban architects, it blends perfectly into the tropical ambience. Palms, ferns and exotic plants spread their multicolored foliage even inside the walls of the hotel itself. Furnished with all modern conveniences, the Marazul also has a large, well-kept outdoor swimming pool for those who are neither beach *aficianados* nor sun worshippers.

While we were there, the winter tourist season had not yet fully opened, so that not all the hotel's 300-plus rooms were occupied. We were assured, however, that all Cuba's resort hotels would soon be full, despite Reagan's noxious ban against U.S. tourism to Cuba. A first large group of Canadians was already there, their northern pallors swiftly giving way to skin shades ranging from pink to red and brown. Numerous other such groups were scheduled to arrive shortly. A Cuban told us in jest that soon there would be so many Canadians at resort hotels that Cuba could be mistaken for a Canadian province, or the other way around. We also met tourists from the Scandinavian countries and Eastern Europe.

The beautiful beach seemed to be enjoyed only by foreign tourists. Cubans decidedly favored the pool. It reminded me of Noel Coward's words that only mad dogs and Englishmen venture out in the midday sun. In Cuba, perhaps only mad foreigners venture into the wintry sea. Yet for us the water was a delight, neither hot nor cold.

The hotel's dining room was of ballroom size, easily seating 300 people at a time, most of them at tables for four. Meals were either a la carte or buffet. Helen and I preferred the buffet, not so much for the variety of cold and hot dishes to choose from, or the temptation to come back for more, but because it saved time. In Cuba, as in other countries where people are not accustomed to or disdain our own fast-food misculture, one can grow old waiting for a meal to be served. As our stay at Marazul was not primarily to taste its finer cuisine, and as there was much documentary material to plow through, we ate a la carte only when talking "business" with Olga, Fernando, Nancy or others.

One day we rented a tandem bike for a dollar an hour and Helen and I leisurely surveyed the area over both paved and dirt roads until the noon sun and hunger drove us to the dining room. Another day we tried the pool. The only other occupants were children. Their parents lovingly watched them while stretched out on beach chairs, often with a bottle of beer in one hand and a cigarette in the other. Cubans, it seems, are great *aficianados* of beer and, unfortunately, many of them are still addicted to cigarettes. I also spotted a bottle of cola, but Reagan need not get upset, it was labeled "Cubacola." Most of the children in the pool wore flippers. Were flippers that plentiful? The probable answer came a day later. The room from which we rented our bike also rented all sorts of swimming, diving and fishing gear at very moderate prices.

Olga visited us on our second day at the Marazul. She was of average height with blond hair and blue eyes, more Nordic than Cuban in appearance. Nancy came with her. Although Olga was studying English, she was far too self-conscious to try testing it on us—at first. She was a young-looking forty years; the mother of three, aged twenty, fourteen and three.

Soft-spoken and businesslike, Olga informed us that she had read my memorandum and had already begun to line up appointments, subject, of course, to our approval. She listed the government ministries and the organizations and institutions she had already reached, and those she still planned to contact. She also suggested that we take a trip to Cienfuegos Province. We added a few more to her list and mentioned the possibility of visiting the Isle of Pines, now known as the Isle of Youth. We put particular stress on a desire to spend time with ordinary people, from whom, we felt, we could often get a somewhat different view on things. Olga readily agreed, assuring us that this was her view as well, but that it did not require advance organization. She urged us to feel completely free to speak with whomever we wished and wherever we happened to be, and to ask whatever questions we desired.

She proposed that we leave the Marazul early Tuesday morning in time to make a 9:00 a.m. appointment with the director of Cuba's Central Economic Planning Board.

Our permanent base of operations became the Riviera Hotel in Havana, even when we took trips out of town.

2. Economic warfare

Among the documents Fernando brought us to read was one of particular importance—an in-depth review of Cuba's economic situation. Issued by the National Bank of Cuba in August 1982, it covered 27 tabloid-size newsprint pages. *El Informe Económico* began by tracing the background of current problems. It pointed out that Cuba, a small, underdeveloped island, totally lacking in energy resources and many other critical raw materials, is dependent upon foreign trade for survival. Prior to the revolution, more than 75% of such trade was with the U.S., in a relationship of inequality and subservience for Cuba. In exchange for a U.S. agreement to purchase a stated yearly quota of Cuba's sugar crop—its main export commodity—free entree had been guaranteed without any protective measures whatever, for all U.S. industrial and agricultural goods. Thus, unable to compete successfully with products coming from the vastly superior productive power of the U.S., this could only perpetuate for Cuba a relationship based on humiliating economic dependence and backwardness.

It found reflection in the way people lived. From twenty to thirty percent of workers, depending on the season of the year, were jobless; forty percent of Cubans over ten years of age were illiterate. Where there were rural schools, most children did not go beyond the fourth grade. There was but one rural hospital with only ten beds, and life expectancy at birth was under sixty years.

This was the "prosperity" that Reagan claimed for pre-revolu-

tionary Cuba in his infamous Miami speech. But there *was* prosperity, of course, for the owners of the huge Havana gambling
casinos, the luxury hotels, the private beaches, the drug trade, and
for the U.S. corporations controlling just about everything in
Cuba. There was prosperity as well for the henchmen and hangers-
on of the bloody Batista dictatorship. But for the vast majority of
Cuban people there was unrelenting and cruel poverty and oppression.

Such were the conditions at the time the revolution triumphed on
January 1, 1959. It was not a palace *coup*, as Castro at the time
repeatedly emphasized. It was a *real* revolution, of, by and for the
people. The grip of U.S. corporations over Cuban life was so
complete, however, that even the slightest efforts to initiate change
aroused their hostility and wrath.

Yet revolutionary Cuba was determined to improve the conditions of life of the people and to assert its right to complete national
sovereignty. Nor could one be achieved without the other. As a
consequence, difficulties with U.S. corporate interests and with
Washington swiftly mounted. Before long, efforts to overthrow the
Castro regime were seriously undertaken, as borne out by the Bay of
Pigs misadventure (April, 1961).

The start of economic warfare against Cuba began earlier on July
7, 1960. At one swoop the U.S. Government arbitrarily and uni-
laterally slashed Cuba's sugar quota in the U.S. market by 95
percent—from 740,000 tons a year to 40,000 tons. This was meant to
be the blow that would bring Cuba's leadership to its senses and
show it who was boss. After all, how could Cuba survive without
the U.S. sugar market? But Washington failed to reckon with two
facts: first, the determination of Cuba's leadership and people to be
the masters in their own land at last; second, that there *was* an
alternative market—the Soviet Union and the other socialist countries.

Infuriated at Havana's refusal to knuckle under, Washington
then stepped up its economic warfare, going from one extreme
measure to another.

In September, 1960, it ordered the U.S.-owned nickel works at
Nicaró to cease all operations and to remove all information and
documentation dealing with the technical operation of the plant.

On September 7, 1960, the U.S. imposed a ban on exports to

Cuba. This included all vehicles and vehicle parts, exempting only new passenger cars.

On October 19, 1960, this ban was extended to cover all exports to Cuba with the exception of food, medicine and medical equipment.

On November 10, 1960, all U.S. ships were prohibited from carrying cargo to or from Cuba.

On March 31, 1961 (just before the Bay of Pigs attack in April), Cuba's sugar quota was completely annulled for the entire year. Nine months later this ban was extended to June, 1962.

On July 31, 1961, Cuba's sugar quota was ostentatiously distributed to "more friendly" Latin American countries.

On December 16, 1961, the provisions of the Trading With the Enemy Act were applied to Cuba and a total ban was imposed on *all* exports to it, *including food and medical supplies.*

On February 3, 1962, a complete commercial embargo was imposed against Cuba.

On March 24, 1962, this embargo was extended to all products which in whole or in part contained any material whatever originating in Cuba, even when manufactured in another country.

On October 23, 1962, the U.S. Government declared that it would refuse any assistance to any country that befriended Cuba or permitted its ships to carry cargo to or from Cuba, even when such cargo originated elsewhere.

On July 8, 1963, a strict control was ordered over any possible transfer of assets to Cuba, no matter what they might be, or what their origin. U.S. nationals were prohibited from becoming involved in any transfer of products originating in Cuba, located or being transported from or through Cuba, or manufactured either in whole or part with any substance grown, produced or fabricated in Cuba.

And on July 21, 1966, Washington ordered that all U.S. commercial contracts contain a clause prohibiting the use of any ship, no matter what flag it flew, that had entered a Cuban port after January 1, 1963.

THUS CAN BE SEEN the desperate lengths of the U.S. economic war against Cuba. Its tentacles were meant to reach out to the far corners of the globe to isolate and strangle the new Cuba. Nations were warned against any friendly contact with Cuba. Even if Cuba desperately needed medicines and medical supplies formerly purchased in the U.S., or spare parts for U.S.-built vehicles or production machinery, no country was to supply these unless it was prepared to risk the wrath and sanctions of the U.S. Government.

This perfidious effort to starve another nation into submission has continued for 23 years without letup. As remarked earlier, it would have succeeded, but for the revolutionary unity and tenacity of the Cuban people and the timely and decisive aid of the Soviet Union. Of great importance, but not to the same degree, has been the refusal of other capitalist nations, particularly Mexico, to bow to dictation from Washington.

It is estimated by the Bank of Cuba that the U.S. blockade has cost the Cuban people $9 billion. This is a huge sum for a small developing country. Yet the cost in human terms far outweighs the monetary cost. How Cuba, especially in those first arduous years without even spare parts for its machinery, was able to hold things together and then begin the difficult advance upwards, is among the great sagas of history.

3. Progress and problems

What is the present state of Cuba's economy? According to the August, 1982 *Informe* of Cuba's national bank, later corroborated by Felino Quesada, the Director of Cuba's Central Economic Planning Board, the year 1981 was the very best economic year since the revolution. Cuba's Gross National Product (GNP) rose by 12 percent.*

This is a notable achievement, notwithstanding the fact that the prior year, 1980, was quite poor. Three important branches of Cuba's agriculture were struck almost simultaneously by virus-infective diseases—its sugar, tobacco, and hogs. Cubans are convinced that these plagues were not due to natural causes but were the result of CIA biological warfare, aimed at crippling Cuba's economy. (We will say more about this later.)

In judging Cuba's economic performance, therefore, a look at a somewhat longer time span is necessary. During the 1970s, Cuba's GNP in constant prices rose by an average of six percent a year, or twice that of the previous decade. Investments during the '70s grew by twelve percent a year, personal income by three percent, and real income, which includes social benefits in addition to wages, by five percent. Thus Cuba's economy has shown steady growth.

*The GNP in Cuba is measured somewhat differently from the U.S. GNP, which is the *total* national U.S. output of goods *and* services. In Cuba, however, the GNP excludes services considered nonproductive such as education, health, culture and administration.

This has enabled a considerable rise in the standard of living. There is now a far greater variety of goods available, especially protein foods, better housing, more and higher quality clothing, and a marked increase in durable goods. In 1975 only a third of homes with electricity (there are still outlying mountainous areas without it) owned television sets; in 1980, three out of four did. Ownership of home refrigerators increased from 15% to 38%, washing machines from 6% to 34%, and homes with radios from 42% to 105%.

Unfortunately, there are still shortages and many things are rationed. When we were in Cuba in 1970, just about everything sold was rationed. Now it is the other way around. Of all foods available, twenty-five percent are still rationed, and of industrial goods, twenty percent.

Rationing is still seen as necessary to make sure that everyone receives a just share of essential needs. Meat production, for example, is still not large enough to enable every family to buy all it wants. Thus there is a danger, if there were no rationing, that families with somewhat higher income, or with less mouths to feed, would get more than their just share of meat.

This is quite different from the situation in capitalist countries, even in poor underdeveloped ones where mass hunger and poverty prevail. The stores bulge with goods to sell of every variety, but usually a majority of the people do not have the money with which to buy. On the surface, by just looking at the displays in store windows, everything seems to be prosperous, yet the opposite is the case. This is true of the United States as well, with its many millions of jobless, its thousands of homeless, and its slum and ghetto poor.

From a capitalist point of view, socialist Cuba's prime concern to meet the basic needs of all is simply crazy. Profit is the name of the capitalist game, and some shortages are all to the good. Prices can be raised and profits increased. What could be better? But as Humberto Pérez, the President of Cuba's central planning board said, "Under socialism that is not the point and that is not what our economic policy is about. Our economic policy and our social system are about people, and making sure that they all get the necessities, even though it brings in less profit and less apparent abundance. We are not interested in appearances but in reality."

With the majority of products no longer rationed, two new types of markets have arisen: a "free market" and a "parallel market". The free market is where one can buy products that are in ample supply, in whatever quantity desired. In 1969 and 1970, eggs were rationed at three eggs per person, per week. Today the supply of eggs seems limitless. The same is true of dairy and many other products.

The parallel market is different. While open to all, it offers scarce and higher quality products at considerably higher prices. This includes both certain types of food as well as rare handicrafts and some industrial goods. The prices in this market, distinct from the other two, are controlled by supply and demand. Its purpose is to complement the rationed and free markets and to give workers a greater material incentive to increase productivity, so that they can earn more to spend in the parallel market. This helps increase production as a whole and therefore the supply of goods for everyone.

DURING THE SECOND HALF of the '70s, Cuba's yearly GNP rate of growth declined to four percent. This was a respectable rate of growth which even developed capitalist countries found hard to reach or maintain in those years. The chief cause for the Cuban decline, according to the Bank's report, was the catastrophic and unprecedented fall in capitalist world sugar prices.Contributing factors were the continued capitalist inflation, especially in prices of manufactured goods, and the unheard-of rise in interest rates. In other words, the main causes of the decline stem from the effects of crisis conditions in the capitalist world and its market and not from a crisis in Cuba's socialist form of production.

With sugar as Cuba's main export, the fall in sugar prices had an immediate adverse effect on Cuba's ability to purchase essential needs from capitalist countries as well as to make payments on its foreign debt. Cuba has been shielded from the most devastating effects of this situation only because of its close commercial ties with the Soviet Union and the other socialist countries. As one of the CMEA countries (Council for Mutual Economic Assistance), Cuba enjoys preferential credit terms and foreign trade prices, as do Vietnam and Mongolia, within the CMEA framework. Had this not been the case, Cuba's position, as is true of so many other developing countries today, would indeed be desperate, even more so in the face of the intense hostility of the U.S. Government and its continuing economic blockade.

Cuba sells about sixty percent of its sugar exports to the Soviet Union and the other CMEA countries. The price it receives from them is adjusted regularly to take into account any rise in the cost of manufactured goods. Part of the payment is in convertible currency; that is, in currency accepted by capitalist countries.

But the portion of its sugar crop sold to the capitalist countries faces an entirely different situation. With the exception of the two years 1974 and 1980, the price of sugar in the capitalist world market has headed downward. Price fluctuations have been so erratic that it is extremely difficult to plan ahead. When Cuba's current five year plan was drafted in 1980, the price of sugar had reached a high of 28¢ a pound; within a few months it had plunged to less than 7½¢ a pound.

Yet the capitalist market has been of importance to Cuba. It has provided hard currency to buy capital goods and certain raw materials not readily available from socialist countries. It also provides means by which to repay the loans and credits acquired during the years when massive capital investments were so decisive to counter the effects of the economic blockade.

Cuban investment in a large maritime fleet is but one example. Before the revolution Cuba lacked a merchant fleet of its own. Its total cargo capacity in 1959 amounted to only 60,000 tons. Like Puerto Rico today, Cuba was at the complete mercy of U.S. shipping lines. To break the economic blockade, Cuba was compelled to build its own merchant fleet. By 1981, Cuba possessed 99 maritime vessels with a total cargo capacity of over a million tons. In time, she further weakened the blockade by renting ships from countries which refused to abide by the U.S. orders. Thus there were good reasons for Cuba to borrow heavily from capitalist sources for a number of years.

New factors, however, make it imperative for Cuba to reduce such purchases, at least for some years. First, Cuba already has a sizable debt to Western banks of over $2½ billion. This is small compared to the $700 billion owed by Third World countries, but it is still too large. Second, what Cuba earns in convertible currency needs to go first of all to reduce that debt and, in time, to liquidate it. The exhorbitant interest rates of recent years have often made such loans counter-productive. It is a way by which developing countries and some socialist countries have been made to pay extortionist tribute to Western banks.

This is in sharp contrast to loans and credits obtained from the Soviet Union and the CMEA countries. These have an amortization span of twelve years, and interest rates never exceed four percent. When loans from the Soviet Union are made for the purchase of manufacturing equipment, payment on these begins the following year. If complete factories are bought, payment and interest start two years after the plant is in operation. Outright financial loans from the Soviet Union have a 25-year amortization period and bear only a two percent rate of interest.

Another factor in this equation is the pressure exerted by the Reagan Administration upon Western banking interests to foreclose on Cuba's short-term loans. As Cuba is determined not to default on its debts, it has no recourse other than to act decisively. Thus a policy of austerity has been in effect for over a year, the objective of which is to cut back on all critical Western purchases. This will mean a somewhat slower rate of growth for a period of time. The growth rate for 1982 was 2½ percent and the same is projected for 1983. But the overall growth rate for nineteen Latin American countries in 1982 was a negative one percent (-1%).

The Cuban people have been made fully aware of the reasons for the conscious decision to hold back from large-scale purchases in the West and have been warned of its possible effects. But the Cubans we talked with, many of them ordinary citizens, expressed confidence that the worst years are behind them and that their great gains in living standards will be maintained and improved.

4. Planning as an art

F elino Quesada (Director of the central planning board) is in his mid-thirties with neatly combed dark hair, a somewhat dapper appearance, and an air of supreme self-confidence. After introducing ourselves and exchanging pleasantries, I explained that we had read the National Bank of Cuba's economic *Informe* and so had some knowledge of Cuba's economic situation. It would probably be best, I went on to say, if we started right in by asking questions. He agreed.

My first one related to a recent document issued by the Joint-Economic Committee of the U.S. Congress, "Cuba Faces the Economic Realities of the 1980s." This credits Cuba with a number of achievements (I quoted the document):

A highly egalitarian redistribution of income that has eliminated almost all malnutrition, particularly among children.

Establishment of a national health care program that is superior in the Third World and rivals that of numerous developed countries.

Near total elimination of illiteracy and a highly developed multilevel educational system.

Development of a relatively well-disciplined and motivated population with a strong sense of national identification.

"But," I added, "these laudatory remarks are buried in an estimate that is highly negative respecting Cuba's future prospects." I then read further:

> In some areas, Castro's social successes have themselves generated growing economic problems. For example, the Cuban economy is increasingly incapable of producing jobs for the relatively well-educated, rapidly growing labor force.

"In other words," I said, "this document indicates that unemployment is now a problem, and a growing one, in Cuba. Is this so?"

Quesada paused for a moment and then replied: "Full employment is never an absolute, nor can it be. There is always some labor turnover, for multiple reasons. There may also develop at times a shortage of labor in one place and a surplus in another. These are easily adjusted. But there is no unemployment in Cuba in the sense of a reserve army of jobless. Those that are briefly without work until adjustments are made do not suffer for this; they are amply compensated." He then spoke of the sugarcane industry. All loading, he pointed out, is now mechanized, as is more than half of all cane-cutting. "Yet we still have to muster an additional labor force of 100,000 at harvest time by taking workers off other jobs. Would this be necessary if we had unemployment?"

Quesada likewise rejected the very notion that there could be a surplus of well-educated young people. There may be at times an excess in a given specialty, he said, "but we are still short of highly-educated, well-trained and technically qualified personnel, and we believe we shall never have too many educated people. In fact, we are spending more on education each year, although we have been compelled to cut back on other expenditures.

"Can we have," he asked rhetorically, "too many teachers or doctors? We now have one doctor for every 600 persons, about the same ratio as in the U.S., but we are not satisfied. We can still use more. And we can also do more to help poorer countries which desperately need good doctors."

I then asked about labor productivity, once again referring to the Congressional committee's report that characterized it as dismal. Quesada agreed that labor productivity could be higher, but insisted it was rising steadily. The Bank of Cuba's *Informe* showed labor productivity rising from less than 4/10 of 1% a year for the decade of the sixties, to over 4% a year for the seventies.

Quesada cited the sugar industry as example once again. Total production had been rising yearly with the exception of 1980, the year of the sugarcane blight. Yet these results were obtained with a steadily lower consumption of fuel oil. In 1970, 350,000 cane-cutters were needed at harvest time; in 1981, only 110,000. These results came from mechanization, improved labor productivity and management efficiency. Also, a byproduct of sugar cane, bagasse, is now increasingly being used as fuel and as raw material in the manufacture of paper and fiber board.

With sugarcane production so often referred to, I decided to ask a question that had troubled me for some time. According to the Bank's *Informe*, I said, the price of sugar on the capitalist market has fallen so low that its return is only about 55% of production costs. "Why then," I asked, "the stress in your plan on increased sugar production? Do you expect the price of sugar to rise? I can understand Cuba's desire to increase its volume of sugar sales to make up for the low price received per pound. At the same time, I realize that increased mechanization will further reduce your production costs. But with the present sugar glut in the (capitalist) world market, it is also possible that any large increase in Cuban output could tilt the price still lower. Isn't there a contradiction here?"

Quesada listened attentively and then replied. First, the demand for Cuban sugar in socialist countries has by no means reached its limits. Cuba has not sold more there because a sizable portion of its crop had to be sold to the West in order to earn more convertible exchange. The price paid by socialist countries, however, takes into account and exceeds Cuba's cost of production.

Secondly, he stressed, sugar remains Cuba's largest source of foreign exchange. It is also a natural source, he argued, renewed each year with little need for new, large-scale capital investments, especially when mechanization is completed.

Then he asked smilingly, "Do you think we can compete with General Motors or Ford? Remember, we also export nickel and many other products, but sugar remains our best export commodity."

"How does this relate to your goal of economic diversification?" I asked.

"It helps make it possible," was his reply. "Cuba is now producing things it could not before. We make our own machines and machine parts for the sugar mills. We have even built a complete mill from scratch and sold it to another developing country, supplying the technicians to help install and operate it. Cuba now has a steel and metal industry. It has modern fishing and citrus industries, builds its own combines, washing machines and televisions and has begun to produce buses. Moreover, the proportion of sugar in our total exports is not rising, but falling. In 1975, for instance, sugar was ninety percent of all Cuban exports to non-socialist countries; in the period from 1977 to 1981, it was sixty-two percent.

My next questions pertained to the work of the planning board. I noted that Cuba has shown considerable and consistent growth, but that it has never fully met the specific objectives in its plans. I wanted to know why more general goals were not set instead of such detailed specific ones. I pointed out that there were too many uncontrollable and unknowable factors involved—the wild fluctuation in sugar prices, the possibility of devastating hurricanes and droughts not infrequent in Cuba's climate, and so forth. The pinpointing of objectives that remain unfulfilled, I argued, could lead to cynicism, with some people saying, "Ah, everyone knows these goals won't be reached."

Quesada's response was that an economic plan must have concrete, specific goals. "Of course, if we had to deal with our country alone, it would be relatively simple. We can say today, for example, and with complete assurance, that by 1985 we will be producing ten million tons of sugar a year. All the factors involved in this are in our hands. But in respect to those not in our hands, such as those you mentioned, it is a different matter. Yet we can't build socialism without numerical goals and objectives, and without the masses striving to reach them, even though the capitalists may say we have failed if one goal or another is not completely met."

He concluded by telling us that Cuba had learned a great deal since 1970, the year of the failed ten million ton sugar campaign. "We no longer plan for sugar alone, but for the entire economy. We also constantly reevaluate where we're at and do not hesitate to make public adjustments in specific goals if that becomes necessary. We did this in 1976 when the sudden fall in sugar prices made clear that we could not reach many of the goals we had set for 1980. Thus, we are not inflexible."

HOW DOES SOCIALIST Cuba know what to produce, in what quantities, and whether these conform to the public's needs and likes? Given a shortage of most things, this is no problem—nearly everything will sell. But with shortages being overcome, how does production take into account changing needs, styles and tastes?

A partial answer to these questions came from an interview with Eugenio R. Balari, president of *El Instituto Cubano de Investigaciones y Orientación de la Demanda Interna.* Dr. Balari explained to us that the institute did social and economic research on material and cultural needs. It supplies information to the Council of Ministers and the Central Economic Planning Board. Its objective is to help establish a proper balance between production and consumption.

Among the tools it uses are public opinion polls, panels, samplings, and concrete investigations of consumer likes, dislikes, habits and styles. "In other words," Balari said, "we try to include the subjective element into objective planning; to bring the consumer to the planners' drawing board."

The institute has branches around the country, a national network of 10,000 families for testing and sampling purposes, and a thousand workers at stores and shopping centers who report twice a month on what people buy and ask for. This information provides the basis for the institute's regular reports to those responsible for planning decisions.

Needs are studied with both long term and short term considerations, Balari explained. The institute also tries to influence public habits and tastes. As example, he cited the current intensive campaign, conducted jointly with the Ministry of Health, against smoking and obesity. *Opina,* the institute's extremely popular magazine, is used to solicit public views as well as to influence them.

Working with the Ministry of Domestic Trade, the institute also tries to bring about a more flexible approach to rationing, which is constantly undergoing changes. Until 1971, according to Balari, about 94 *centavos* out of every consumer *peso* was spent for rationed goods. Today, it is only 40 *centavos*. Also, from 1970 to 1980, wages increased by 107% not counting the social wage—the over three million lunches served in schools and work places, the subsidized transportation and housing, the free sports, educational and health facilities, etc. Thus, something of an imbalance developed between wages and prices, because prices had not been increased since 1965. However, some adjustments upward in prices were made last year, but far less than the rise in wages.

"Our function is mainly research," Balari said in summary, "we do not make policy. We provide the information needed to make it."

5. Cutting red tape

On my visit to Cuba in 1969, I interviewed Blas Roca, then chairman of a special government commission drafting a new Cuban constitution. (My acquaintance with Roca, too, dated from the years of his leadership in the Popular Socialist Party, the old communist party.) At that time, our animated talk had touched on many subjects, and first of all on the work of this commission.

I had asked him when the draft of the new constitution would be finished. He replied that they were making haste slowly; they did not wish to write a document which only incorporated the best of existing constitutions. "Our constitution must be Cuban, tailored to fit our own reality and guarantee a truly democratic government and judicial system." For this reason, he said, they needed time to test certain propositions in actual experience before incorporating them into a document as durable as a constitution. He described a new law already in effect. It established a system of people's courts, where lay judges, elected by the people of a community, dispensed justice.

On this visit to Cuba we again spent time with Blas Roca. The new constitution had been drafted, altered further in the course of public debate, and adopted by popular referendum on February 15, 1976. Blas Roca was pleased with the results and with the public acclaim accorded it. Although the new electoral system had been in effect but six years, he was convinced that it had already proved to be thoroughly democratic. He did not claim perfection for it. Wisely, he knew that as time passed further improvements and changes would be made.

We were greatly interested in learning all we could about the new electoral system and what exactly was meant by the term "Peoples Power." Even before interviewing Blas Roca (we saw him near the end of our visit), we had asked people wherever we went about the new electoral and parliamentary system. We had also read much literature on the subject, had met with leaders of the National Assembly in Havana, with members of the Cienfuegos Municipal Assembly, and had attended a regular session of the Cienfuegos Assembly. From all this we had gotten a fair overview of Peoples Power and how it worked.

Two preliminary steps had been taken before the new system was put into effect; in fact, before the new constitution itself was finally adopted. The first aimed at simplifying and greatly reducing the bureaucratic overlapping that characterized the then existing political-administrative structure. The second put the new electoral system to a prior test in Matanzas Province before adopting it nationally. It is important at this point to say something about the first of these.

In 1878, under Spanish colonial rule, Cuba had been arbitrarily divided into six provinces and 132 municipalities. (A Cuban province is roughly comparable to a U.S. state, although without the latter's historic setting and powers. A Cuban municipality is comparable to our own county form of government. Its geographic area usually consists of both towns and countryside, although it can also be limited to one metropolitan area or subdivisions of it.)

Nearly a century later, Cuba was still divided into the same six provinces. Yet much had changed. In 1878, Oriente Province (at the extreme east of the island) and Matanzas Province (in the northwest) were approximately equal in population. But by 1970, Oriente had six times the population of Matanzas. To bring about greater decentralization and closer contact with the municipalities, 58 regional administrative bodies were interspersed between the provinces and the municipalities in 1963. In that same period, a wild increase in the number of municipalities also took place. It seemed as though even the smallest hamlet had decided to put on long pants and call itself a municipality. Thus, four separate levels of administrative authority existed—national, provincial, regional and municipal. In turn, this led to what Cubans aptly term *empleomania*, the bureaucratic tendency to meet a problem by throwing more paid personnel at it. Yet of the 200,000 or more employees engaged in administrative and auxiliary services, fully 38% were at the regional level and only 16% at the municipal.

This called for substantial change, but where and how to begin? After a lengthy study of the problem, locality by locality, and numerous discussions at all levels, the following decisions were made: to completely eliminate the regional setups; to increase the number of municipalities to 169; and to increase the number of provinces from six to fourteen. The aim of these proposals was to adjust the provinces and municipalities to more uniform criteria of area, population, resources, services and transportation. Great disparities would continue to exist, of course, yet an approach toward greater balance was essential, if only from the view of more equitable relations within the new electoral and governmental structure.

To make changes as original as these, touching on people's sensitivities to their native region and its borders, required an extremely high degree of social awareness. The interests of the whole had to take precedence over feelings of local provincialism. It was as if we, in the U.S., considered ending an electoral system in which each of our states is entitled to two seats in the U.S. Senate, though Delaware, for example, has less than 2 million inhabitants and California more than 24 million. But Cuba has a decided advantage over us. It lacks the private corporate interests that stand to gain or lose if representation is based more squarely on population.

The decision to alter the administrative structure would have been more difficult were it not for the previous testing of the electoral and Peoples Power system in Matanzas Province. This experience showed how to interrelate centralism and decentralism. It showed that obtaining the maximum participation of people in the running of local government, could also provide the mechanism for maximum control over government at the higher provincial and national levels. It also proved to be the most effective way to reduce excess administrative personnel and bureaucracy.

6. How Peoples Power works

Cuba's governmental structure resembles a pyramid. At its base are the 169 Municipal Assemblies; halfway up are the 14 Provincial Assemblies, and at its peak, the National Assembly.

Delegates to the Municipal Assembly are elected by direct popular vote from designated assembly districts or, as often called, constituencies. But those elected to the Provincial Assemblies and the National Assembly are not chosen by direct popular vote. Instead, they are elected by their respective Municipal Assemblies on a proportional basis. Deputies of the National Assembly, for example, are chosen on a ratio of one for every 20,000 inhabitants or the major fraction thereof.

Thus, the Municipal Assemblies are the local form of government but also something more. They are the foundation upon which rests the entire governmental structure. In this way each level of the assembly pyramid relates back to its base. It is what Cuban's mean by Peoples Power.

This electoral system is obviously different from that in the U.S. Here, members of city councils, state legislatures and the U.S. Congress are all elected by direct popular vote. Why the difference in Cuba? They believe that their system is superior for them because it makes more difficult a hierarchical separation of national and provincial government from local government and the people, and it enables more effective control from below over all branches of government. The Cubans refer to their system as one of "double subordination." The lower levels of government are subordinate to the higher ones, but those in the higher rungs of responsibility are, in turn, subordinate and strictly accountable to those who elected them and can be recalled at any time.

There is another important difference. Cuban Assemblies at each level combine both legislative and executive functions. The National Assembly, for example, as Cuba's highest contitutional authority, elects from its ranks a National Council, a Prime Minister, and the Council of Ministers; that is, the executive arm of government. The Administration, as we would call it, is responsible to the National Assembly for its policies and actions.

To understand how Cuba's election and governmental system works in practice it is necessary to take a closer look at it. Let us start at the bottom. We had an opportunity to do this in Cienfuegos, a growing commercial and industrial community about 200 miles southeast of Havana. While there we met with members of the Cienfuegos Municipal Assembly. Luis González, the Secretary of the Assembly, explained how it was elected.

The municipality of about 125,000 people is roughly divided into 79 population districts. Each is entitled to one assembly delegate. The first step in an election is nomination. To enable a maximum participation in nominating, each district is subdivided into still smaller neighborhood areas. Special meetings are convened in these areas where a voter may simply rise and nominate a candidate. Only those 16 years of age and over (voting in Cuba begins at 16), and who live in the election district may be nominated. The one who gets the highest vote is the area's nominee.

There is one stricture, however. Organizations as such are prohibited from either nominating or supporting a candidate. The election, González assured us, is strictly nonpartisan. Obviously, many Communists sit in the Assembly as delegates, "but they are all nominated and elected strictly on their personal records and merits, not on their organizational affiliation." The vote at the neighborhood nominating meeting is by a show of hands; a majority is needed for nomination.

The next step is preparation for the actual election. As neighborhood nominating meetings can choose someone from the district who does not live in their own area, the number of candidates is often less than the number of area nominating meetings held.

According to election law, however, there must be no less than two and no more than eight candidates on the final election ballot. (Apparently the district is divided so that there are no more than eight separate nominating meetings.)

Once the candidates are known, their biographies and photographs, all of the same length and size, are given widespread circulation in the entire constituency, via press, posters, radio, etc. Each candidate, by law, must receive equal exposure; no more, no less. No candidate, individual, group of individuals or organizations, can put out material for one candidate and thus give him or her a publicity edge. As a nominee from one area may not be known in other parts of the district, meetings are held at which the record and qualifications of such candidates can be presented.

Final voting takes place at designated polling places throughout the district. After identification, a voter enters an election booth and casts a secret ballot. The ballot box is guarded by a group of neighborhood children, eight to eleven years of age. Children also give aid to handicapped and older people. If no candidate receives a majority vote, a runoff election is held between the two runner-ups.

We then asked González to describe how the Assembly gets down to work. A constitutional provision, he told us, determines how sessions open. The oldest elected delegate comes forward and after saying a few words occupies the presiding officer's chair. He remains at that post until regular officers are elected by the Assembly. The three youngest delegates act as his secretarial assistants. "In this way," González said, "we honor age and youth at the same time."

The first act of the Assembly is the election of an Executive Committee of eight. This includes a President, Deputy President and Secretary. In effect, the Executive Committee is the administrative body of the municipality. The number of full-time Executive Committee members is discretionary, but in Cienfuegos, all eight were such. The other 71 delegates continued on their regular jobs, receiving their regular pay for the time spent on official duties as members of the Assembly.

Each Executive Committee member assumes personal responsibility for a group of municipal departments. Each department has its own director, a person professionally qualified in a field such as health, housing, education, transportation, community services or in the running of the many different kinds of municipally owned industrial and commercial enterprises. When an Executive Committee member in whose jurisdiction a certain department falls believes it necessary to replace the director, the Executive Committee has the authority to do so, but provisionally. Final approval or disapproval must come from the next regular session of the Assembly. "At tomorrow's session," González informed us, "we are proposing the replacement of three directors. There have been too many complaints about the malfunction of their departments."

When I later mentioned this to a person not a member of the Assembly, he remarked that, at least in his opinion, there is often too great a rush to replace a director under fire. "A department's poor functioning is sometimes due to other causes—a lack of material or skilled labor, or more general difficulties associated with overcoming defects and habits of the past. But," he mused philosophically, "when a change of directors does not bring the desired results, a search for more basic causes has to take place."

While unable to judge the accuracy of this observation, we did get some idea of the pressures involved. We had asked other Executive Committee members present at the interview to describe the most recent of their obligatory twice-yearly constituency meetings.

Delby García is the delegate of constituency No. 41. It has 1,243 eligible voters, of whom 87% attended one or the other of the two separate meetings held in different areas of his election district. García said that he delivered a written report to these meetings on the work of the Assembly and on his own efforts to meet proposals and criticisms made at previous constituency meetings. These related to many things: street repairs, bus service, the need for more house paint (given free by the municipality); the request for an additional supermarket in the district, for a special school for children with behavioral problems, for more home-building materials; and complaints about the rudeness of some bus drivers and city employees.

Ciro Ramón Alvarez is the delegate of constituency No. 14. At one of his meetings, 1,100 voters were present; at the other, 245. Together, these represented approximately 80% of the electorate. To indicate his knowledge of the constituency, Alvarez mentioned that he had run three times for Assembly delegate, losing the first election, winning the second, and then reelected. Questions raised at his meetings varied somewhat from those in district No. 41. Voters, he said, were angry that building materials unloaded on a beach had left it cluttered with debris. They wanted it cleaned up. Citizens in one area of the district complained that the water pressure was too weak. Others complained that buses tended to fill up at the first stops, leaving no room for passengers further up the line. They wanted the buses rerouted so that not all of them started from the same place. There were also complaints that the buses were dirty on the outside although the municipality pays workers to keep them clean. And so on.

When we asked Alvarez if he *was* able to satisfy constituency complaints, he said that fully 93 percent of those made at a previous constituency meeting had been resolved satisfactorily. This claim seemed high to us in face of the motley demands made. Yet he must have done some things right to be reelected. In addition to these mandatory twice-yearly constituency meetings, each Assembly delegate is required to spend one full day a week meeting with people in his district. He must also be available day or night in case of emergency.

As a member of the Assembly's Executive Committee, Alvarez also heads its commission on public services. This is composed of Assembly delegates and individuals directly involved in one or another branch of public service—markets, hotels, restaurants, and the other types of retail and wholesale enterprises. The control over local enterprises, he assured us, "is very tight," with regular inspections taking place. He had recently visited every shopping center in the municipality to check things personally.

THE NEXT MORNING, Saturday, we attended the regular session of the Cienfuegos Assembly. It met in the large hall of the *Primer Palacio,* a handsome 19th Century structure, now the permanent seat of the local Peoples Power. The hall was on the ground floor; its doors and windows faced *Parque Marti,* one of the most beautiful squares we had ever seen. The delegates occupied the front center section of the hall, each seated at a desk-type mahogany table with a shelf below for documents. Visitors sat in graceful hardwood chairs at the rear and sides. The session was public; anyone could enter and be seated.

The session opened promptly at 9:00 a.m. (We arrived late, after an earlier visit to the provincial hospital.) The hall was full, except for the seats which had been reserved for us. We had missed the first order of business, the report of the Executive Committee, which had been discussed and acted upon. We were told that the Assembly must approve, reject or amend a report of the Executive Committee.

By the time we were seated and began listening to the debate, delegates were reporting on those matters from their recent constituency meetings which required Assembly action. One delegate told of criticisms leveled at the public utility. It was accused of overcharging. The meters, it was claimed, were either not registering properly or those sent to read them didn't know their business. This opened a more general criticism. One delegate complained that when a new housing development was occupied, the electricity was not turned on in time. Another, that meters are sometimes read every few months instead of monthly, thus making families pay too much at one time.

We were also told that the Assembly is required to take some action on every problem placed before it. Usually the President, as presiding officer, suggests how the problem should be met, and by what date. In this case he proposed that the utility commission be instructed to respond to the criticisms within a specified time. He added that the problem should be raised with the provincial authority as well, for electric power is transmitted from outside the municipality.

Still another delegate reported that people had complained about chickens being sold while frozen, which weighed considerably less when thawed. And so it went. After awhile we lost interest. To us, these seemed trivial matters, although obviously they were not trivial to those who raised them.

The next point on the agenda was the election of 45 municipal judges, 42 as lay judges and three as "professional judges". The lay candidates were workers, housewives, doctors, teachers, engineers and students. The professional candidates were lawyers. All of them had been nominated by people in their communities or at work centers. Being elected a judge was considered a great honor.

Each candidate rose as his or her name was called, walked to the front of the hall and turned to face the delegates. As each was announced, we saw delegates shuffling papers as if to refresh their memories about that candidate. The judges were to be elected for 2½ year terms, but while the professional judges served that entire period, the lay judges served only two months each. We were told that one professional judge sits with two lay judges, providing greater legal knowledge and courtroom experience. Before serving, lay judges attend special courses to prepare them for their responsibilities.

Later, during an Assembly recess, the delegates lined up in an adjacent chamber to cast secret ballots for the judicial candidates of their choice.

7. Cuba's parliament

Among those present at our interview with deputies of the National Assembly were Dr. Luis Yodu Prevez, the National Assembly's legal counsel and Rafael Fernández, the head of its foreign affairs committee.

We were first briefed on the National Assembly's role as the highest constitutional authority, the seat of national legislation and the body that elects the executive branch of government. If any valid comparison at all can be made, Cuba's National Assembly is, in one respect at least, more like the British Parliament which chooses the Prime Minister, than the U.S. Congress (which has no direct power over the President except through impeachment for malfeasance in office).

All deputies must, in the words of the constitution, "render account of their activities any time the Assembly deems it necessary," and are subject to recall by the voters. The constitution also states that being a deputy "does not entail personal privileges or economic benefits of any kind."

The National Assembly is required to hold three regular sessions a year and special sessions when requested by one-third of the deputies or by the Administration. The National Assembly elected in 1981 was composed of 494 deputies, of whom 113 were women. The deputies were divided into sixteen functioning commissions. New legislation is proposed in a variety of ways: by individual deputies, groups of deputies, the Administration, Assembly commissions, mass organizations, the Supreme Court, the Ministry of Justice, or can emanate directly from citizens who submit petitions with 20,000 or more signatures.

An initial draft of proposed legislation is sent to all deputies and heads of important people's organizations for their opinions. A final draft must reach each deputy at least twenty-five days before it is to be debated and acted upon. Adoption is by simple majority. A constitutional amendment, however, requires a two-thirds majority. If a proposed amendment infringes on the duties of the National Assembly or its administrative bodies, or on the rights of citizens, it must be submitted to a national plebiscite. Other legislation deemed important enough may also be submitted to popular referendum, as has already occurred a few times.

Even before the new constitution was adopted (1976), a Family Code was submitted in 1975 to public debate and vote. The Code received lively, often passionate, discussion because it dealt with highly sensitive relations between the sexes and between spouses, and with the age-old curse of male supremacy.

Since then, a new Penal Code, a Code on Children and Youth, and a new Social Security Law have also been submitted to public perusal and referenda. Dr. Prevez assured us that the people made many changes in them. More than 2,000 additions, deletions or amendments were submitted to the Penal Code, resulting in vital alterations in 46 of its Articles. The Social Security Law, he said, had been discussed "nearly word for word in more than 46,000 union and workshop meetings."

We asked about the recall provisions of the constitution. "Were these real, or just formal rights never exercised?"

"They are real," we were told. In the first election under the new constitution, in 1976, more than 30,000 candidates ran for delegates to the Municipal Assemblies. Of these, 10,725 were elected to 2½ year terms. By the end of that period, 114 had been recalled by their constituencies. Of the 481 deputies elected to the National Assembly in 1976, four had been recalled. The recall procedure is simple: A majority vote at a constituency meeting, whether regular or special, automatically compels a secret-ballot vote of the entire electorate. Furthermore, no one can be removed from elective office except by those who elected them.

One feature of the Cuban electoral system seemed strange to us.

Candidates do not run on programs or issues, but exclusively on their records. Yet in the States we demand that candidates state where they stand on issues, even when we know that most of them will not live up to their pre-election promises. Why the difference in Cuba?

The Cubans we asked, including the three deputies interviewed, answered: "Our situation is different from that in the U.S. We do not have a capitalist class against which we must unceasingly struggle to win some concessions. Here, if there's a yearly average 4% rise in personal income, it's 4% across the board, not 10% for some and nothing for others.

"I know," I'd reply, "but are there not issues over which people may honestly disagree? Is there only one way to meet a problem or to decide which problem gets priority? And what about mistakes? Are socialist countries immune to them, even grave ones?"

"Of course mistakes can be and are made," was the usual reply, "but we do not want our elections to degenerate into candidates competing over promises, or scurrying for issues with the purpose of snaring the most votes. That is fakery. We believe our way is better. If people vote for someone they really know, whose life and record is an open book, they can have confidence that they will be served faithfully. And remember, there is always the right to recall."

"Yes," I said, "that is true, but what about honest mistakes, how can they be corrected?" The invariable answer was that adequate means exist for correction. They pointed once again to their mandatory twice-yearly constituent assemblies, where people speak their minds freely, criticize and make proposals. They referred to other grass root-type assemblies as well, at work centers and local unions; of students, farmers, women, neighborhood, or block meetings of the Committees for the Defense of the Revolution (CDR). All of these, they said, were forums for public debate.

One woman told us of her work place assembly, "It's amazing how many different questions get raised from the floor and how free the discussion is, especially on the most disputed questions."

Another person spoke of the philosophical aspect: "We do not wish to encourage personal egotism by emphasizing what a single individual may accomplish; it is what the Cuban people as a whole can attain by their collective will, labor and struggle."

None of those we spoke with were arrogant or dogmatic in

defense of their electoral Peoples Power system. They were sure that in time there would be further improvements. In fact, a public discussion had already begun with that end in mind.

A major contribution to it is a book *La Organización Estatal en Cuba,* written by Domingo García Cárdenas, a member of the commision that drafted the constitution and its electoral provisions. Blas Roca (who headed the commission) wrote a laudatory introduction to this book. García believes that even in the short period since Peoples Power was instituted in 1976, it has proved to be highly democratic and efficacious. Yet he makes criticisms of how it functions.

He believes that there is still "an excessive centralization" of decision making. Some people, he writes, defend this on the ground that there is still a lack of qualified personnel at lower administrative levels. García does not quarrel with this, but stresses the need for a more conscious effort at greater decentralization. Higher administrative bodies, he says, are frequently buried in mountains of documents and try to make decisions on matters that really belong, and can better be handled, at lower levels. He also points to an inadequate use of available scientific and technical expertise.

García is critical of the methods by which many of the Municipal Assemblies function. He believes that their Executive Committees do not plan sessions adequately to focus the most attention on the most important questions. Some things are done merely for the record, as when commissions make "largely artificial" reports of the number of meetings held and the agendas, but raise no important questions for Assembly discussion and action. This, he observes, "arouses interest in no one," and wastes precious Assembly time.

From our own admittedly brief observation, we feel that García's criticisms have validity. The delegate constituency reports at the Cienfuegos Municipal Assembly that we attended were largely pro forma. While they accurately reported the criticisms made of one or another municipal department, these could have been raised directly, without first coming to the full chamber. As it was, the Assembly referred most of them back to such commissions and departments anyway.

One person we talked with agreed that there were too many problems placed on the shoulders of Assembly delegates. Many of

them, he believed, could be better handled by encouraging people
to raise them directly with the given responsible agency, whether by
phone, letter, or delegation. When so much time of delegates and
Assembly sessions is taken up with routine and less important
problems, it stands to reason that the really important ones will fall
to the province of the higher, more centralized administrative
bodies. It may also be that an Assembly cannot do full justice to its
responsibilities with sessions so few and so short.

García made other criticisms as well, all of them going in the
direction of combatting still existing tendencies of *"el papaleo* (red
tape), *"el peloteo,"* (buck passing), and "insensitivity and bureaucracy."

8. Entitlements, Cuban style

One recalls the proud assertion of our own Declaration of Independence that governments are instituted among men to secure their inalienable rights to life, liberty and the pursuit of happiness. While it has been honored more in the breach than the observance, especially for racial minorities, women and the working class, it did proclaim "inalienable rights." Now the very opposite is taking place. The present position of the U.S. Government, as stated by President Reagan's budget chief, David Stockman, is that the people have no entitlements; have no claim on government.

Not so in Cuba. The Cuban socialist government believes that the people have rights and entitlements. The new Social Security Law, in effect since January 1, 1980, states that the responsibility of the government is to meet ever more fully the material and spiritual needs of the people and that a first objective is guaranteeing the right to life, health, education and social security.

Cuba's concept of social security goes far beyond our own. It affects *every* Cuban directly and immediately; in one form or another, they are all recipients. No person out of work, unable to work, or retired, is without means of livelihood. No sick person is without adequate medical care. No child, youth, or adult, is without means of schooling, higher education and self-development. In other words, social security in Cuba is an array of entitlements, financed and guaranteed by the government.

Immensely impressed by what we had seen in Cuba in 1969 and 1970, we wanted to know what changes had taken place in its social security system since then. When we first arrived, we were given a copy of the new Social Security Law and a number of booklets describing its various features. Olga also arranged an interview for us with Francisco Penalver García, the Deputy President of Cuba's State Committee on Labor and Social Security. But because social security is so interwoven with all aspects of social life, we learned more and more about how it operates and its immense role from the people we talked with, and in just about every place and institution we visited.

The agency of which Francisco Penalver García is Deputy President, functions in a dual capacity. It protects labor's rights under the law as well as directing the social security system. These functions frequently overlap, as can be seen by Title I, Article 2, of the new Social Security Law. It reads:

> The system of social security protects the worker in cases of illness (whether on or off a job), maternity, disability, old age, or in the case of death provides protection for the worker's family.

More than workers are protected. Title I, Article 1, states that "the government guarantees protection to the worker and his family, *and to the general population*" (emphasis added). This latter designation includes people no longer able to work, retired, or who, for one reason or another find themselves unable to cope without public assistance.

Grants to beneficiaries are made in three ways; in services, in kind, and in money. The services, entirely free, include medical and dental care, preventive and curative; hospitalization, general and specialized; and physical and psychiatric rehabilitation. Grants in kind, also free, include medicine, both in and out of hospitals, and orthopedic equipment in case of accident or physical deformity. Monetary grants are given in cases of illness or accident such as pensions for total and partial disability; for retirement; and in the case of a worker's death, as pensions to the surviving dependents. Children are covered up to age 17, but continue receiving their benefits if still in school.

We were given a number of examples on how the social security system works. Retirement pensions are different for those who worked under normal conditions than for those employed under greater physical or mental stress, such as "miners, pilots and teamsters." In the first category, men can retire at 60 years, and women at 55. In the second category, men can retire at 55, and women at 50. The amount of each pension is determined by the years of employment. A worker who has worked 25 years starts out with 50% of the former annual salary. This percentage rises with every year worked beyond 25 years.

Workers totally or partially handicapped receive pensions based on their years of employment and their medical condition. If partially handicapped, a worker may be shifted to another job, "so that, for example, someone who cannot work standing up is given a job sitting down." If this new job pays less, the difference is made up by social security.

"What if a worker has been unemployed or ill for long periods," I asked, "as was the case with unemployment prior to the revolution? Is that time deducted from his record of working years, or counted in his or her favor?"

"Yes, it is true that before the revolution workers had long periods of unemployment. But as long as a worker had been idle through no fault of his own, the dead time (as we call it) is still counted as working time and credited to him."

"But if a worker has had employment for far less than 25 years, or sporadically, as is often the case with women who have children, how can they live on such meager pensions?"

You must remember," Penalver replied, "that people have no medical, dental or hospital costs to worry about. Moreover, rents range from 6 percent to 10 percent of earnings; not, mind you, of the family's total earnings, but of its member with the highest earnings. In cases where there is a problem, our social security system contains within it an extra social assistance provision. Therefore those who cannot manage on what they earn or receive are entitled to supplementary assistance. At present, there are about 127,000 such cases."

For example, people who receive what is known as "short-term pensions" may fall into this category. A person who is hospitalized receives, in addition to free hospital care, from 50 percent to 70 percent of weekly earnings, depending on whether illness or injury took place on the job or under other conditions. Likewise, if the worker is ill or injured but staying at home, he is entitled to from 60 percent to 80 percent of the regular pay. Should this be insufficient to tide the family over, it can receive supplemental aid.

Maternity leave is also in the category of short-term pensions. When we were in Cuba in 1969 and 1970, expectant mothers were entitled to twelve weeks of maternity leave at full pay. The new law has extended maternity leave to eighteen weeks, six before birth and twelve after. No expectant mother is permitted to continue working after the 34th week of pregnancy. This is to "guarantee that the unborn child gains in weight and development." Should a child arrive later than the expected date, the law permits up to two additional weeks of maternity leave at full pay. Also, for the first year of the child's life, the law gives the mother one day off per month without loss of pay to take the infant to the pediatrician.

Every Cuban worker is now guaranteed a full 30-day vacation annually, at full pay. As a consequence, we found Cubans extremely vacation conscious. But like every advance in life, this too has its problems. Previously, workers thought of vacation time as the hot months (I should really say, the hottest months) and the place for it, the beaches. But to let everyone off a full month during the same short season is obviously impossible. Yet most Cubans will not immerse even a big toe in the ocean at any other time.

Fidel has personally promoted camping, and a group of highly prestigious literati recently took a hiking trip into the Sierra wilderness, visiting historic sites such as the spot where Jose Martí was killed, and eloquently and lovingly describing in rhapsodic prose the beauty of what they had "discovered." With such stimulus, camping has suddenly come into its own. Camping sites are being constructed as way stations and places to buy food and other necessities. Thus for some, vacation time is becoming a back-to-nature time.

9. The home of Santa Susana

Near the outskirts of Havana our car turned into a driveway that, from the looks of the spacious, well-kept grounds, belonged to a mansion. It turned out to be a Catholic-run home for the aged. The large brick building, surrounded by a porch, was built in 1886. It had been transformed from a monastery into a *casa asilo*, a home for old people, through a donation from a very wealthy woman. The salon was filled with her 19th century over-stuffed furniture; a tall, handsome grandfather clock, and a large oil painting of the donor (since christened Santa Susana) on a wall.

As we entered the home, we were greeted by its director, Mother Superior Guadalupe García, wearing her nun's habit. She suggested we tour the home first, asking questions as we went along. There would be ample time for additional queries afterward.

The home had 406 residents and about 100 nuns and maintenance personnel. The house was huge, with long, wide corridors, high ceilings, and multiple rooms. Some residents were busy with tasks. Others sat on chairs or rockers reading, chatting, knitting or just sunning. There were two wings, one for men, the other for women. In each of these were dormitories, with beds neatly made and lined up, with chests of drawers for personal belongings.

Married couples lived in one-room apartments. We asked permission to enter one and saw a bed, stove, small refrigerator, television, and table and chairs. We were told that many couples had brought their own furniture. While there were large televisions that could be

watched by all, those in the apartments were privately owned as
were the refrigerators. We asked whether they did their own cooking. "It depends," was the answer, "sometimes we want to eat by
ourselves; at other times, in the dining room."

"Do you pay anything for living here?"

"No, we give 80% of our retirement pension to the home, but it is
not compulsory."

"Do you prefer living here to living with your family?" Helen
asked.

"Yes," the woman answered, "that's why we're here. It's nice,
quiet, clean, and we can even keep our own pets. We see members of
our family frequently; they visit us or we visit them."

"You leave here for such visits?"

"Oh, yes," and then with a twinkle in her eyes added, "and
sometimes we go into town for a spree. We leave and return as we
please."

The home had an immaculate kitchen with recently arrived new
cooking equipment, and a large, modern laundry. Outdoors we saw
where ducks, turkeys and rabbits were raised. The specialty was
rabbits. We assumed it was because they multiply rapidly. "No, that
is not the reason," we were told. "A rabbit's meat is softer, less
sinewy and more digestible than fowl or other meats. Many people
here are very old; they prefer rabbit meat." There were also two
sheep on the grounds. As no one had mentioned sheep raising,
Helen surmised that they served as four-legged lawn mowers. The
only fruit cultivated was bananas. Vegetables and other fruits were
bought in town or rabbits and bananas were bartered for them.

Back in the building, we stopped at a room in which a woman
with a tape was measuring the girth of an older woman. Along one
wall was a long clothing rack with dresses. On the other side were
shelves piled high with bolts of cloth of various colors and designs.
At a table, a woman with scissors in hand was cutting cloth along a
paper pattern. On an outdoor patio adjoining the room, four or five
women sat at sewing machines.

The women working here had been seamstresses or sewn at
home. For them, sewing was a form of creative self-expression, done
for pleasure and at leisure. Every female resident was entitled to a
new dress a couple of times a year. They could choose from five
different styles and whatever colors or quality of cloth was availa-

ble. A nun accompanying us said, "We do not want our older people to wear only house smocks. We want them to be able to dress up, as they did in the past. It is important for morale and self-respect."

"What about the men?" we asked.

"They are not left out. There is another room in which men's trousers and *guayaberas* (Cuban style shirt-jackets) are made."

The last room we visited was the dining hall. It resembled a commercial restaurant, with tables for four and a vase of freshly-cut flowers on each. "They choose their own seating arrangements," we were told.

The tour over, the Mother Superior greeted us again, and asked for our impressions over cups of freshly ground Cuban coffee. We thanked her, expressed pleasant surprise at what we had seen, and began our questions:

"Can someone who is a non-Catholic live here?" This question had occured to us a number of times as we went from room to room seeing crucifixes on the walls, statuettes and pictures of Christ in corridors and salons, and reading notices on the bulletin board about morning mass and Sunday services.

"We ask no one what their religion is, or if they have one," the Mother Superior replied. "This home is open for anyone in retirement, as long as we have available space."

"Yet this is a Catholic institution, is it not?"

"Yes, it is, and we who serve here belong to a special international order of nuns."

"To operate a place like this must cost a large sum of money. Is the church prepared to do this also for non-Catholics?"

"No, the Church does not finance us."

"But you can't maintain this home just on what you get from pensions!"

"You are right, what we get from them is inconsequential. It goes for fringe items, such as the new clothes you saw being made. It also goes for outings. Once a year they even go to the Tropicana night club. It means much to them, but the cost comes from their contributions."

"Then how are you financed?" I asked.

"The government gives us a lump sum every three months as operating expenses. In addition, we get 420 liters of milk daily, for in Cuba every child and old person is entitled to a liter of milk every day. The municipal government takes care of all costs of building and machine maintenance, and any new construction."

Having previously been told that the elderly get good medical and dental care, we asked, "Why are some without teeth?"

Smilingly she explained, "As you know, many very old people find it difficult to wear dentures. They use them only for eating. If you looked you would find them in their bedroom drawers. We take excellent care of their health. There was a time when it was customary to say, 'They're old, why operate on them?' But now, no matter how old a person is, our objective is to extend each life."

"What about senility? How do you cope with that?"

"First of all, we try to prevent it by keeping our residents active, involved with others, and in close touch with their families. Those who are unable to get along on their own live upstairs. They are cared for by nurses."

She stressed that close contact with families was a priority. When an older person applies for admission, there is first an attempt to help him or her remain in the family unit. If this proves impractical, they are placed in a senior home as close to family members as possible. Should there be no room in the nearest one, they are sent somewhat farther off, but moved closer as soon as a vacancy occurs.

We also learned that the Santa Susana *casa asilo* was not exceptional, but that most are not church-run. There are not yet enough of them to fill the need. "But as you can see," the Mother Superior assured us, "our government is constantly working to meet such needs."

10. Change in wage policy

In 1969, I visited a new textile mill in the small town of Gibara, in Oriente Province. It was a modern, air-conditioned plant, employing 272 workers. After making the rounds, I interviewed the factory manager in the presence of five or six workers. At one point in our conversation I asked, "Would you mind telling me what your salary is?" Surprised, he pointed to his revolutionary record, insisted that he had no interest in making money, and that the honor of being chosen plant manager was more than enough. "But since you've asked, I'll tell you—I earn 142 pesos a month." Then pointing to a man standing in the doorway he said, "That comrade is the plant sweeper; he makes 138 pesos a month."

I tell this story for a reason. Had I visited the mill on my latest trip, I'm sure I would have found a greater wage differential between manager and sweeper. An important change in policy has taken place in the interim.

We discussed this matter with two top leaders of the *Central de Trabajadores de Cuba* (CTC), the Cuban Federation of Labor. Francisco Travieso is the CTC's National Director of Organization and a member of its Secretariat. Manuel Montero is a member of its International Relations Department.

"Prior to 1970," Travieso told us, "there was very little difference in the wage scales between workers. Often a worker with little skill would be making as much as someone with high technical qualifications. Also, a worker who shirked job responsibilities, or

came to work only a few days a week, could earn nearly as much as
one who worked conscientiously all week. The shirkers may have
been relatively few, but permitting this situation to exist had a
demoralizing effect."

Now, however, Travieso continued, Cuba has learned how cor-
rect the observation of Karl Marx was, made more than a century
ago, and confirmed by socialist experience since then. In his
booklet *Critique of the Gotha Program,* Marx warned against
romanticism. The new society as it emerges from the womb of the
old, he wrote, cannot at first fully meet the needs of all. Marx
foresaw two stages; the first, lasting a considerable period, would
end exploitation and guarantee that workers received back from
society the equivalent of what their physical and mental labors had
contributed. But in the "highest stage" of the new society (communism), when labor is no longer a drudgery and "all the springs of
cooperative wealth flow more abundantly," it will be possible to
meet fully the needs of all, irrespective of individual capacities and
contributions to society.

In talking with a Cuban friend about this later, he defended the
earlier policy of wage equalization as unavoidable. The workers
had to learn from their own experiences that income equalization
could not come all at once, he argued. Furthermore, even had more
money been given to those with greater qualifications, there was (at
that time) nothing they could buy with it. Times were very hard and
just about everything available was rationed. Nor could Cuba let
anyone go hungry or homeless, even shirkers. So what good was
extra money? He believes, however, that one mistake was made,
"We turned a temporary necessity into a virtue. Now things are
different."

But not entirely different. There are still shortages and some
things are very hard to get. That is why the rationing of essential
commodities at government-subsidized prices is still in effect, so
that no one goes without them.

There may be some truth to the observation that the earlier policy
was inevitable, but Fidel has frankly admitted that in those first
years a certain romanticism took over. Nor is this surprising when
one considers how a valiant few, led by Castro, began an armed
struggle against what seemed to be overwhelming odds, won the
working class and peasantry to its side and emerged victorious.

"Is there not a danger that some people may now make a virtue of the new wage policy?" I asked my Cuban friend.

"Yes," he replied, "there is always a danger of swinging to opposite extremes. And there is no doubt that some petty bureaucrats could use this to justify a craving for special privileges. But the top leadership, I am certain, is well aware of this danger. It places moral questions in the forefront. Our heroes are not those who earn more, but those who do more and sacrifice more, who go to teach and cure people in jungles of faraway lands, and who in every other way exemplify the high moral stature of our revolution. I am sure you've seen ample evidence of that."

Another aspect of the wage question was touched on by Francisco Travieso at our interview in the offices of the labor federation. He pointed out that a Cuban worker receives two types of wages; a direct wage for actual work performed and an indirect *social* wage which he gets irrespective of work performance. "We know, of course, that there are countries with wages higher than here, but one needs to take into account our social wage—the many benefits workers receive, such as minimal rent, free health care, free education, a month's vacation with pay, eighteen weeks of maternity leave with pay, and numerous other benefits as well."

When Travieso said that the many entitlements are "free," he meant that people were not directly charged for them. But their cost must still come from the total wealth produced by the workers' labor, as do corporation profits in capitalist countries. In the last analysis, therefore, Cuban workers do "pay" for these benefits by receiving less in their pay envelopes.

There are important reasons why Cuba and other socialist countries prefer this sort of double wage rather than concentrating all earnings in the pay envelope. First, it guarantees that everyone and every family, no matter what they earn, receive in full and equal measure those services decisive for life, health, education and well-being. Second, it indicates how they envision the future and the gradual transition to a communist society.

In the early years of the Cuban revolution there were attempts to make additional services free of charge. These included rent, telephone calls and electricity. But the level of mass social consciousness was not yet high enough to ensure that everyone would use these facilities responsibly, in a non-wasteful manner. Hence fees were re-imposed, but just high enough to exercise some control over how these resources are used. Telephone calls and bus fares are five centavos (5¢); admission is free to athletic and many cultural events.

In time, as the productive forces of socialist society greatly expand, it is envisioned that more and more material goods and cultural facilities will become free of charge, until only those that are still scarce are paid for directly, or another and better way is found to determine their distribution.

Already many things are distributed according to need, not income. Around 1970, for example, a new movement arose among workers for the construction of homes in order to help relieve the housing shortage. It became known as the "mini-brigade" movement. Some workers were released from their regular jobs (but with the same pay) to build housing for the workers of their factory. The workers who remained in the factory organized their work to fill the gaps left by the mini-brigade members so as to maintain production levels.

By 1978 there were at least a thousand such construction brigades with a total of over 26,000 workers. From 1974 to 1978, more than 51,000 new structures were built in this way. The Alamar housing complex, occupying a vast area on the outskirts of Havana, is a striking example of the professional level attained by these brigades. At Alamar we became lost in a huge forest of new high-rise buildings, housing some 40,000 people. The apartments in such new housing units do not go only to the builders. The workers of a plant collectively decide which families are to get them.

11. Union democracy

A vast expansion of the Cuban labor movement has taken place since our 1970 visit. There is no longer a questioning of the need for a trade union movement in socialist society and its important role is generally recognized. Travieso told us that there are now 18 trade unions in the country, all affiliated to the CTC. Practically speaking, all workers are members of unions, even though membership is voluntary. The CTC has close to 2½ million workers in its ranks, 98% of the entire work force. Its role is to defend the rights of the workers, as well as to participate actively in management. In addition to union assemblies, there are monthly workplace assemblies at which workers discuss problems of production and management and make their proposals or criticisms. Unions are represented on industry-wide management boards.

The labor movement plays an important political role. Before being acted upon, every piece of new legislation is first submitted to the CTC for its judgment and suggestions. On specific labor legislation, the CTC is the prime mover and has the decisive influence. Travieso referred to a recently adopted salary reform law that was first discussed throughout the labor movement. This law established the legal basis for wage policy and also raised total wages by 670 million pesos a year, with the largest increases going to the lowest paid workers.

In the past year, a law on occupational health and safety was also adopted. The unions take the responsibility for its enforcement.

The CTC has set itself the objective of training 50,000 workers as technically qualified inspectors by 1985. In addition, all workers are receiving special instructions in safety. There is great concern to increase health and safety in the workplace, for accidents have been relatively high, particularly in agriculture, sugar production and construction.

In explaining what he called the CTC's "democratic mechanisms," Travieso first stressed that the CTC and its affiliated unions are neither party nor state organizations. He quoted from the CTC's Statutes which state that it is an autonomous mass organization whose principles and policies are determined exclusively by its membership.

While emphasizing the CTC's autonomous character, Travieso made clear that it recognizes the leading role of the Communist Party in the building of socialist society and works in the spirit of "working class internationalism."

Travieso told us that of 261,000 elected local union executive board members, 41,000 were members of the Communist Party, or approximately 16%. The percentage was much higher in the upper ranks of leadership, he said, but no one is elected or not elected because of CP membership. "They are elected on the basis of their records and the confidence that the workers have in their integrity, ability and policies." He also stated that Party members (he is one) do not function as a faction within the unions and do not support slates of candidates. "The Party's role is ideological. Obviously, its members convey the Party's general views, but in no way does the Party organization interfere in the internal affairs or the democracy of the unions."

In discussing this matter with others, and in particular with Fernando García, the young man who first met us upon our arrival in Cuba, there was constant reiteration that the Party is scrupulous in its respect for the autonomy of the mass organizations. Fernando referred me to the Statutes of the Party, adopted at its last congress, which state that the CP recognizes the organic independence of the mass organizations and seeks to exercise its leading role by means of the fullest and most democratic discussion with them and by total respect for their autonomy.

As an example of the unity in CTC ranks and its internal democracy, we were referred to the published *Proceedings* of the recent CTC Congress, its 14th. They confirmed that the basic document (thesis) submitted to the congress was first discussed at local union assemblies throughout the country. More than 1,800,000 workers participated in 44,356 assemblies. Each of the document's 13 sections was discussed and voted upon separately. The result, carried in the *Proceedings,* indicated that only 4,909 votes were cast against one or another section of the document, and that 12,015 abstained. There were also 24,395 proposals made, apparently as amendments. There were 275,168 *"intervenciones,"* that is, workers who spoke from the floor in these assembly discussions.

It is hard to believe that only 17,000 votes were cast either against or in abstention, out of 1.8 million participants. Nor do we know how thorough the discussion was, or the atmosphere, in the many thousands of assemblies that were held. It is also possible that some disagreement took a passive form. Yet the facts indicate that this important policy document was submitted to the entire membership for discussion, section by section, and that there was a serious attempt to find out how the rank and file felt about it.

In his summary at the 14th Congress of the CTC, its President, Roberto Veiga Menéndez, said:

> The thesis of this congress, debated fully by the workers and supported by the overwhelming majority, was previously the object of a long process of study and elaboration, participated in by nearly the totality of our cadre across the country. Thus, our thesis was the result of the collective thinking of our cadre and of the workers.

> The essence of the main report rendered here, particularly its projections, were based on the thesis and the results of the discussions at the conventions of our 18 affiliated unions, as well as at the municipal and provincial conferences. That is why the largest number of those who spoke here on the main report, identified with it.

It is interesting to note, in passing, what questions drew the largest number of contrary votes and abstentions at the assembly meetings. The largest number were on the section dealing with economic problems. The next largest, in order, were on matters concerning voluntary labor, housing, and women. The section dealing with trade union democracy had only 101 contrary votes and 555 abstentions. These vote totals may roughly indicate those questions on which the greatest differences exist.

IT DID NOT SURPRISE us that there was still some disagreement on the role and rights of women. When we asked Travieso what role women played in the labor movement, he told us that women now make up nearly 30% of the work force and are a majority in some unions. "We have been striving for a greater representation of women in economic, political and social life, and we are making headway, but there is still much to be done. Of the 261,000 members on local union executive boards, 117,000 are now women, about 45%. But as we go higher in the union structure, the percentage falls. On municipal and provincial union executive bodies, the percentage of women is 31%, but for national posts, it is only 18%."

"What explains the disparity?"

"Well, it is not easy to win the battle for women in top leadership positions. First, there is the old curse of *machismo,* of men resisting the idea of women in leadership. They may not voice these views openly at meetings, but they vote that way on their secret ballots. Another problem is that some of the women turn down national responsibilities for traditional reasons—the age-old habit of women taking second place. There are other factors, too. Women still bear the main responsibility for children and the home. They hesitate to assume tasks that will take them away from home too often. Yet national responsibilities require attendance at board meetings and conferences, visiting areas away from home, public speaking, and so forth. And there is also the factor that while it takes a number of years to reach the top, the great influx of women into industry and unions has been more recent. All these problems complicate matters, but we are determined to continue making headway."

Our last question was on how union leaders were elected. We were told that all leaders, from local union to the highest post in national leadership, must first be elected from their own work centers and local unions.

Local union elections take place every 2½ years at regularly convened local union assemblies. Prior to the actual election, the outgoing leadership renders an account of its stewardship, an elected auditing committee reports its findings, and an election committee is chosen. Nominations are made from the floor. The final vote is by secret ballot on which there must be more than one candidate for each office.

The same essential procedure is followed in the election of delegates to all higher union bodies, including delegates to national union conventions. In respect to representation at a CTC Congress, however, the procedure differs, for it is impossible to have direct representation from more than 40,000 local unions. In this case, therefore, the election is indirect, with each affiliated national union allocated delegates in proportion to its membership. These are chosen at conferences of local union delegates at municipal and provincial levels.

In all elections there is an attempt to adhere to the principles of renovation and continuity. Thus we were told that there was a 54% turnover in the most recent local union elections, and a 45% turnover in the CTC election.

Another principle strictly adhered to at all levels is the right to recall an elected official whenever a loss of confidence occurs. This right can be exercised only by the original body which elected the official.

Summing up, Travieso said: "All members of the CTC's National Secretariat (its highest body), were first elected in their work centers, then in their territories and provinces, and finally at the last CTC Congress. And yes, even our election to the Secretariat was by secret ballot."

Then he added, "I am convinced that what happened in Poland could never happen here. Our ties with the workers are so close, the treatment of our country's problems so different, that it is inconceivable that we could ever face such a situation. There apparently had been no real freedom for union activities there, but in Cuba we have the mechanism for the fullest participation of the masses. We never have had as high a level of union participation and democracy as we do today."

12. Is there a doctor on the block?

The report of the Joint-Economic Committee of the U.S. Congress on Cuba, cited earlier, acknowledges that Cuba has established a national health care program superior to any in the Third World and rivaling that in developed countries. From this it draws the dismal conclusion that "Castro's social successes have themselves generated growing economic problems."

Public health investment is a costly undertaking for a small, developing country like Cuba. But the Cubans consider it the very best investment they can make. Castro has reiterated that Cuba does not expect to be a great economic or military power, but it does intend to be a great medical and cultural power.

Cuba's progress in the field of health is an immensely dramatic story, in sharp contrast to our own government's slashing of health funds without regard for its human consequences.* To get this story, we interviewed Dr. Vicente Osorio, the Director of the Ministry of Public Health, and Prof. Armando Alvarez, his assistant.

Prof. Alvarez, with charts and slides to illustrate his points, first

---

*A Washington dispatch in the *New York Times* of January 17, 1983 indicates what these cuts are doing to mothers and children. "In the last 18 months, every state has reduced health services for poor people, especially women and children. . . . Almost 700,000 children lost coverage under Medicaid . . . infant mortality rates are rising in Alabama, Maine, Michigan and Ohio . . . 47 states made cutbacks in maternal and child health programs . . . funds for health centers have been reduced by 13 percent . . . 44 states reduced prenatal and delivery services to pregnant women or preventive health services for children . . ." etc.

reminded us of the health situation before the revolution. There was no public health system; no accurate health records were kept, nothing was done in preventive medicine, and all medical services were private. The only medical school in the country was in Havana, and at least half of its 300-plus graduates a year left for the United States. It is known that infant mortality was high, abortion the main cause of maternal death, and that many people died of tuberculosis, malaria and diphtheria. Venereal diseases were widespread and uncontrolled.

Changes came with the Revolution. A Ministry of Health was established on the following principles: that health care is a human right and a responsibility of government; that all medical services are free; that these must be integral, dealing with the relationship of cure to prevention, treatment to environment, and physical problems to social ones.

The Ministry organized its work on four geographic levels; national, regional, provincial and direct aid. When the government structure was improved in 1976, the Ministry made corresponding changes. It divided the country into 358 health districts, each with 25,000 to 35,000 inhabitants. In these districts polyclinics have been established to handle health care, hygiene, dentistry, social assistance and daycare nurseries.

Medical service is divided into three specialties: pediatrics, gynecology and internal medicine. Only in sparsely populated areas is one doctor responsible for all three.

By 1981 there were 391 polyclinics throughout the country and three different types of hospitals; for children, for pregnancy, and for clinical and surgical care. There are 44 hospitals in Havana, a few of them specializing in psychiatric, orthopedic and ontological care. There are also 212 first aid stations throughout the country.

Fifty-two hospitals are located in remote rural areas, mainly mountainous; rural areas close enough to cities use the urban facilities. Because of the variety of health problems encountered in the countryside, all medical students and interns are expected to spend a year at rural hospitals.

In 1958, there were no clinics or institutions for dentistry; today there are 137 with an integral treatment including surgery, orthodontia, dentures, root canal work and preventive care. Dentists are available at polyclinics for special attention to children. There are now 67 modern homes for the elderly with more being built in all provinces. There are 17 homes for the physically and mentally handicapped, and more being built. Blood banks were commercial institutions before the revolution; now there are 21, and every hospital has its own bloodbank system. There are 38 laboratories for hygiene and microbiology, and the aim is to have at least one in every municipality. There was but one medical school before the revolution; now there are 14 and by 1985 there will be 24. There are 12 research institutions and special schools in different branches of nursing.

What all this means for the Cuban people is shown by these statistics. Doctor visits increased from 14 million in 1963, to 49 million in 1981. Hospital admissions doubled, from 700,000 to nearly 1,400,000. Dental visits leaped from 200,000 to 10.5 million. And 99% of all births now take place in hospitals. As a result, infant mortality declined from 43 deaths per 1000 live births in 1962, to 18 in 1982 and only 14.2 for the first six months of 1983. Life expectancy increased from 62 years in 1960, to 73.5 years in 1981.

To fully grasp the significance of these figures one need only compare them with the situation in Latin America, not to speak of Africa and Asia. Here are some facts taken at random for the year 1980: Infant mortality per 1000 live births was 96 in the Dominican Republic; 60 in El Salvador; 77 in Bolivia; and 47 in Mexico. Life expectancy was 49 years in Bolivia, 58 years in the Dominican Republic, 58 years in El Salvador, and 65 years in Mexico.

Not a single country in Latin America, even those more economically developed, come close to Cuba in these indicators of life expectancy and health care.

We asked Dr. Osario and Professor Alvarez the main causes of death in Cuba. As in the U.S., they are heart disease and cancer. Malaria cases used to be a runner-up, but now the only incidence has come from abroad. When they began outlining their measures to reduce cancer and heart disease, or to control them when they occur, we found that these were not much different from those used in the United States. For cancer, the emphasis is on early detection when possible, and on finding and eliminating the chemicals and other agencies, industrial or otherwise, that may cause cancer.

Their efforts to reduce heart disease stress combating smoking (which they consider to be a major factor in both heart and lung cancer diseases), reducing the growth in sedentary life by encouraging athletic and physical activities, and changing bad eating habits. Cuba consumes more pork per capita than any other country in Latin America. "We now have a new kind of malnutrition developing," Prof. Alvarez said, "not from lack of food but from overeating."

Our next question related to the terrible dengue fever epidemic that struck Cuba with vehemence in 1981. We wanted to know how they succeeded in overcoming it so rapidly and thoroughly. It was fought as a major battle, we were told, not only by the Ministry of Health, but by every organized force in the country. The fight was led personally by Fidel. The Ministry saw to it that every hospital in Cuba established a separate intensive care section for those suffering from the fever. To eliminate the source of the infection, a mass educational campaign was undertaken. The fever's symptoms, its causes, the specific type of mosquito responsible, and the measures needed to locate and destroy these insects and their eggs were explained to the people. Every possible place where even the slightest quantity of stagnant waters could accumulate was disinfected. Within three months the main battle was won. But it did not stop until there was certainty that a new epidemic could not occur.

Purely by chance, we saw evidence of the thoroughness of this campaign. At the home in which we stayed in Cienfuegos, we noticed a sticker on the inside of the front door. This read:

MINISTERIO DE LA SALUD PUBLICA CAMPAÑA DE ERRADICACION DEL MOSQUITO "AEDES AEGIPTI"

Below the inscription were the six dates when the house had been inspected and sprayed with disinfectant, and by whom. The first date listed was January 9, 1981; the last one was September 19, 1982. Thus the campaign actually lasted, even though with less frequent checks, for more than a year and a half.

Wherever we went, the people were intensely proud of this "war" that they justly felt had been won by their own disciplined and effective struggle. Of all the people we spoke with, there was not a single person who doubted that this contagion did not originate from natural causes, but from the CIA's biological warfare against Cuba.

What we learned at the Ministry of Health was given further

substance when we visited the Gustavo Alderguía Provincial Hospital in Cienfuegos. Two staff physicians, Dr. Luis Quevado and Dr. Luis Antonio Pérez, became our guides.

The Alderguía Hospital had been in existence for three years. It had cost 19 million pesos to build. Architecturally, it was a first of its kind, although now there were two more identical ones. Its location was on the outskirts of town, surrounded by open space with well-kept lawns, trees and flowers. Entering the building, we found ourselves in what could easily have been the large lobby of a tropical hotel.

Our two hosts informed us that the hospital had 130 staff doctors, most of them specialists; 230 registered nurses and 111 nurses in training; 130 laboratory technicians, and 136 other employees. The Alderguía Hospital is a clinical, surgical and teaching center, with 691 beds. Neurosurgery, however, is the specialty of a hospital an hour away.

As a rule, a patient goes first to a polyclinic, and from there, if necessary, to either a municipal hospital or to this one. In emergencies, however, a person can go directly to the hospital's emergency section.

Patients undergoing surgery continue their treatment upon release on an outpatient basis. Where radiology is required, however, they are sent to a hospital in Santa Clara, nearby, which specializes in radiation therapy.

Intensive care varies with the need. One or two nurses are assigned to each patient being monitored. "The cost of a day in intensive care," a doctor told us, "runs as high as 200 pesos, but the patient pays nothing." We also saw patients already up and around, but still cared for in a separate section of the intensive care ward.

The advanced medical technology in use greatly surprised and impressed us. As we passed through a number of the laboratory and diagnostic rooms, Helen, who has had considerable administrative experience in one of the most modern New York hospitals, remarked that the equipment was as good as she had seen. Particularly impressive to us was a large, modern, ultrasound machine recently bought from Japan at a cost of over $100,000. Each of Cuba's 14 provinces has a provincial hospital comparable with this one.

On the day we left Cuba for home, an event took place of great importance for Cuban medicine. The largest and most modern hospital in all of Cuba opened its doors. The Hermanos Ameijieras Hospital is located on Havana's famous seafront Malecón Drive, in an imposing 24-story structure. Its construction, and the modern equipment with which it is furnished, cost 60 million pesos. It has 25 operating rooms, 50 rooms for consultations, 17 X-ray units, an emergency ward that can treat 800 people a day, and 50 rooms for outpatient service, capable of handling 1,500 a day. This imposing institution has 950 beds, 2,500 employees, and specializes in 30 different services. Those needing highly specialized diagnostic treatment or therapy will come here from all over the island. The hospital will also serve the 300,000 people in its immediate community (Central and Old Havana).

A new feature in this hospital is its computerization. Each floor has its own computer terminal through which physicians can feed data into the hospital's central computer bank on each patient's health background and present condition. Forty computer programs had already been set up, covering patient admission, discharge or transfer, and up-to-the minute data on each patient's progress.

It had not been idle talk, therefore, when Castro declared in 1980 that Cuba "can become a world center of medicine, capable of exporting its services to many countries and welcoming many people here who need medical aid."

This may prove to be Cuba's most revolutionary export.

The time will come, Castro said in 1983, when we shall have a doctor in every school, workshop and farm enterprise, and ultimately, "a doctor on every block if that is necessary."

13. Facing up to machismo

Of the laws that were first submitted to public perusal and criticism before being adopted, the Family Code was undoubtedly the one most heatedly debated, particularly in the privacy of homes. The reason for this is obvious: it challenged cherished customs and habits of thought with age-old roots. For the first time, the equality of women in marriage was established by law. This equality was further fortified in the Code's Article on the rights and duties of children, declaring that *all* children in a family are equal. Thus was disputed the traditional view that the male child was endowed with the special rights and prerogatives of the father, and the female child, with the second-class status of the mother.

The Code also established the equal rights and duties of husband and wife. Both bear equal responsibility for the upbringing of the children. Both "must participate, to the extent of their capacities and possibilities, in the running of the home. . . ." Both must help meet the needs of the family, "each according to his or her ability and financial status." Both husband and wife have the right to work at their profession or skill, and the duty to help each other toward this end, organizing home life accordingly.

The support of children is legally binding on both parents, even during separation or divorce when the children are not under the direct aegis of one or the other parent. While applicable equally to husband and wife, this provision obviously has special meaning for the mother, who was customarily left with full responsibility for the children.

Parents also have the duty to provide their children with proper nourishment, protection, education and recreation, as well as to raise them as useful citizens with "respect for social property and the property and personal rights of others." Parents can lose custody of their children if they fail to provide for them adequately, are grossly negligent in parental duties, involve the children in crime, or commit crimes against them.

Since its adoption in February 1975, the Code has had a salutary effect on husband-wife relations, and on the overall rights of women and children.

At the neighborhood assembly of a CDR group in Cienfuegos, I asked: "Has the Family Code brought greater equality for women, or is *machismo* as prevalent as ever?" Pedro Pérez Lorenzo, the president of the local group responded by saying that the Code had indeed brought change. When he concluded, I said that I would like to have a woman in the audience answer whether the Code had made a difference in her own life. There was general laughter and I noticed women glancing at one another to see who would rise to the occasion. Finally, one did. She said that the Code had made a great difference in her family life, that her husband had changed; he now shares in household chores, does shopping, and helps with the children. "It has made our marriage stronger." As she spoke, women smiled and nodded in assent and she sat down to considerable applause.

Later, when the dancing started, this woman and her husband introduced themselves and affirmed that what had been said was the truth. Then, as if to prove that things had really changed, she asked me for the honor of the next dance. I accepted, remarking that the honor was mine but the risk was hers.

Yet it would be simplistic to think that a new social system and a new law can in a short period of time erase long-imbedded influences and prejudices. These linger on, sometimes in the open, sometimes in concealed ways; frequently unconsciously, even on the part of people who think they are totally emancipated from the traditional grip of backward and reactionary views. This is true of more than *machismo*. Only those who conceive of the still young socialist system as a utopia, or are disappointed that it is not, fail to understand this. By the time we left Cuba, we saw evidence of an ongoing struggle for women's equality. Its full realization will require further changes in objective conditions and, particularly, in the thinking of men, but also in that of women.

Encouragingly, everywhere we went on this visit to Cuba, there was a greatly heightened consciousness of what is called euphemistically "the woman question." Just about every institution we visited provided us with facts and figures on the number of women employed, or engaged in its activities, and in what roles. Often this was done without our asking, and frequently with explanation that despite efforts, full equality was not yet attained.

From an interview with Nora Quintana, a national leader of the *Federación de Mujeres Cubanas* (FMC), the Cuban Womens Federation, we got an up-to-date picture of what had been done to untie Cuba's "other hand," its women, for the building of the new society and for their own full emancipation.

In my earlier book on Cuba, I reported how difficult it was to get men to accept. . . (nay, to permit!) their wives to leave home for meetings where other men would be present, or to go out alone, and especially to work for a living. At that time one had exclaimed to his bride-to-be, "I am a revolutionist and I work for you and me," refusing to agree that she work after marriage. Another young woman of 19 had written to the magazine *Mujeres*, complaining, "I want to work but my fiance does not let me." Many parents placed the same ban on their daughters, considering a job as tantamount to sexual looseness.

In the main, that day is over. At the time of the revolution, Nora Quintana said, only 13% of Cuban women worked, mainly as domestics. About 100,000 young women were prostitutes. Today, prostitution has been eliminated, and 34% of all women of working age and out of school are employed, not only as workers, but increasingly in skilled professions.

Considerable credit for this is due the FMC which was formed in August 1960. It has become a powerful voice of women, in behalf of their rights and for the attainment of all the other goals of the revolution. At the end of 1982, it had more than two million members, some 81% of all Cuban women fourteen years of age and older. Assemblies (chapters) exist in every locality of the island.

There is little doubt that Cuban women are intensely proud of, and dedicated to, the FMC as *their own* organization. Its record of achievement has won the respect and admiration of men as well. It assumed the immensely difficult task of breaking the subjective barriers that kept women from knowing about, or entering into, the world outside their homes. It also led the way in establishing the first daycare centers for pre-school children, so that working mothers would be assured of proper care for their children. By the end of 1982, there were more than 800 such centers with more being built.

Pioneering effort has characterized the activities of the FMC in all the years of its existence. It has organized an immense network of women's discussion groups, reading and study circles, artistic and cultural activities and events, and special schools for training women leaders. Its National Committee of 94 is made up of women who are outstanding in many fields. Thus great headway has certainly been made.

As with trade unions, women now hold a sizable proportion of elective posts at the lower and middle rungs of political administrative leadership, but very few at the top. Exceptions to this rule are in those organizations or occupations where women predominate.

One reason already discussed is that women have not had the time or experience to rise to the top. This is undoubtedly true in many instances, but certainly not in all. Furthermore, how are women ever to get the experience, if they're kept at tertiary or secondary levels?

Another obstacle was touched on by Olga and Fernando. Both of them are deeply involved in important responsibilities, but were it not for Olga's mother who lives with them, they both could not be as active as they are. It is grandma who helps take care of Ernesto, their beautiful, bright, and highly inquisitive three-year-old when he is sick or on busy evenings or weekends. (He wanted to know why the sun falls into the sea and why my hair starts on top of my head).

Generally, were it not for the grandmas, it would be extremely hard for women to be as active as they presently are, for when it comes to which of the parents stays home with the child, it is usually the mother who does so.

Nor can it be said that the lingering male prejudices against women holding positions from which they "give orders" to men, is entirely something of the past. The other side of this is the still ingrained and submerged fear of many women that if they rise to positions higher than their husbands, it may break up their families.

Thus, even though waning, the old still casts its shadow on the new.

14. Early love

While we walked through the corridors of a countryside boarding school we were visiting, followed by a group of boys and girls in their mid-teens, I asked the woman teacher who was showing us around whether anything was done about sex education. "Yes," she replied, "we have biology classes."

"That's not what I mean," I explained, "I'm sure these youngsters know all about birds and bees and how life is procreated. What I was asking about was the human, social side of the sex relationship."

"We've begun to have conferences on that," she answered.

The way this was said, however, gave me a feeling that for her, at least, sex was a taboo subject, and that if they had really begun to deal with it, they had *just* begun. While her response was symptomatic, it was not typical. We found increasing concern with one aspect of this problem, and for good reason.

In a book given us at the Ministry of Education, reviewing the school year 1981-82, we found a striking fact. Up to twelve years of age, school attendance of the sexes was nearly identical at 97.1% for boys and 97.3% for girls. The less than 3% who did not attend stayed away mainly because of physical or mental problems. But by sixteen years of age a considerable gap had developed—6.5 percent more boys than girls were attending school. This was much more pronounced in rural areas, reaching as high as 20 percent.

One reason for this sex discrepancy is that many parents, especially those on the countryside, still hold on to the old view that "education is not for girls." But the Ministry of Education believes there is also another reason, the high incidence of very young marriages.

Cuba has one of the highest marriage rates in the world, but also one of the highest divorce rates. Just as those getting married are younger than before, so are those getting divorced. This is a problem now getting greater attention.

Cuba's most popular magazine, *Opina* (with a circulation of over 400,000), opened its pages for a discussion of this problem in the October and November issues of 1982. It asked readers: Why such youthful marriages and such rapid divorces?

Editorially, *Opina* stated that one factor in the increase of youthful marriages is economic. The victory of the revolution brought with it a rise in the standard of living and greater general security. "But we must not forget," it adds, "that a multifaceted and complex phenomenon such as marriage is equally influenced by psychological and social factors."

The response of *Opina's* readers indicates that among the causes of early marriage were pregnancy, a desire for independence from parents, and strong cultural influences from the past.

First among the causes mentioned was that of unexpected pregnancies. In such sudden crises, social pressures (particularly those of the immediate family) are exerted which see a precipitous marriage as "the only way out." It is hurriedly consummated to hide from public knowledge what will soon be visible to the naked eye. The "shotgun marriage" is accompanied by bitterness and angry recrimination, and a feeling of shame for "dishonoring the family."

A second cause mentioned is the conscious grasping at marriage as an easy and rapid escape from parental tyranny, or what is considered as such.

A third, the desire to have normal and regular sex relations with the beloved, without the problems, inconveniences and tensions which come from not having a private place where sex fulfillment can take place in dignity.

Another reason was the fear that parents (particularly mothers) instill in their daughters that unless they marry early they could become "old maids." Thus, as in feudal days, love is expected to play little or no part in the young woman's choice.

With such factors helping to cause immature marriages, it is no surprise that so many of them do not last long. The causes of divorce listed by *Opina's* readers were: incompatibility; the attraction of someone else; onerous living conditions, especially when sharing the same domicile with parents. Cuban statistics also show that divorce is not the result of an aversion to marriage as an institution; within an average of five years, those divorced get married again.

An article in *Granma* sums up the situation:

> It is vital that we once and for all free ourselves of the outdated concept of the bourgeois double standard. We cannot expect attitudes and behavior patterns in keeping with a socialist morality if we continue passing on to our children and teenagers different standards for boys and for girls. There are still many parents, however, who teach their sons to "show you are a man" and to "gain a lot of experience" while virtually forcing their daughters to wear chastity belts. How many times can one still hear mothers inculcate their daughters with concepts like submission, passivity, sex discrimination, and the acceptance of the status quo without criticizing their partner's infidelity? Out of ignorance, many women even believe that men "need" more sexual activity than they do and that such sexual activity is "a man's natural privilege."

> For our society, it is an important aim to achieve a gradual reduction in the number of teenage pregnancies and assure that our young people acquire the necessary knowledge for the establishment of love relationships and marriages and raise stable, happy families.

Thus the roots of sex inequality and the male supremacy mentality run deep, and it will take time and persistent, tireless effort to eradicate them completely.

15. Farm cooperative

The farm cooperative we visited had only been in existence for eight months. It's name was *Cooperativa Congreso Campesinos en Armas*. In 1958, months before the victory of the revolution, Fidel and his comrades had convened a congress of peasants in arms, held high in the Sierra, to work out what later became the Agrarian Reform Law that gave land to the landless peasants. The choice of this name was therefore symbolic. It said, in effect, that the cooperative was a continuation on a higher level of the revolutionary movement which had first given them their own land.

We drove through the countryside, passing a few industrial centers as well. To a question about the much enlarged portrait photo posted at the entrance of a textile mill, we were told that the enterprise had been renamed for this 21-year-old martyr, who had worked here and since died in Angola.

We were eager to meet with the farmers to find out, from them, what had induced them to merge their privately-owned farms into a cooperative. After all, hadn't Fidel himself promised that their farms would never be taken from them?

Nearing the place where we were to meet the farm's executive committee, we came upon a cluster of houses and other unpainted buildings on an unpaved street, and Cuban cowboys with big ten gallon hats and heeled boots, riding on small horses that looked like burros. In appearance, they were much like cowboys in our country but smaller, with the same weatherbeaten faces and piercing eyes.

We met seven executive committee members (three of them women) in the cooperative's open air pavilion. They explained to us that their president was ill and had sent his greetings to us, certain that those present could provide us with the information we sought. The committee members were relatively young, with no teenagers but also no gray heads. They looked like typical farmers; hardworking, wiry, not given to many words. The exception was Elsa Rodríguez, a vivacious woman who spoke frequently and eloquently, the others reinforcing her words with nods and interjections.

The co-op had thirty members, of whom eleven were women. There were twenty children. It is a cattle raising and coffee farm; 38 *caballerías* for cattle and 5½ for coffee. A *caballería* is approximately 33 1/3 acres. In the short period of its existence, the co-op had already harvested more than 11,000 bags (28 lbs. each) of coffee and sold 4,000 of them. The co-op had also sold 70 head of cattle out of 220. The men took care of the cattle; the women of the coffee. This division of labor seemed logical to them, for the men had to sit in the saddle for days on end, and sometimes stay away overnight searching for strays. Furthermore, the co-op had not yet had time to build its own day nursery. Most of the families still lived in their scattered homesteads, and it was easier for the women to combine coffee growing with the other chores. Involved also, of course, were matters of traditional lifestyle.

We were told that the co-op members elected their own leaders, made their own production plans, and ran the farm as they saw fit. The cattle and coffee are sold to the state at agreed upon prices. The books are balanced at the end of a given period, and the earnings divided fairly, based on the labor put in by each member. Five percent of total co-op earnings are set aside for social and cultural purposes.

"Why did you decide to merge your farms?" we asked. One of the women replied that they had heard of other peasants forming farm cooperatives and watched with interest the gradual improvement of their standard of living, and the many other social benefits reaped from living and working together, not only for the adults, but for the children. After talking this over among themselves for a long time, they finally decided to take the plunge. They contacted the *Asociación Nacional de Agricultores Pequeños,* (ANAP) the National Association of Small Farmers, to find out how they might start a co-op themselves.

"Were there any pressures on you to take this step?" we asked.

"No," came the chorus of replies, "the decision was entirely ours."

Many of the old folks had not wanted to give up their private land, fearing to start an entirely new kind of life. They were not molested; their desires were respected. Thus, some of the members of the co-op did not bring their family land with them but they were taken in as equals just the same. The private farms still belong to their parents, and will pass into the co-op only after they are gone. We were also told that the co-op movement is the only development that will keep some of the younger generation on the land, for they see no future in the old rural way of life.

While proud of what they have achieved in their short period of collective effort, these co-op farm families are well aware of how much is yet to be done. Most of them still live in their old homes, but hope to move into new ones in a co-op community, within a year. The state has allocated funds for housing construction which can be repaid in 15 to 20 years, without interest.

They already have a primary school and in time expect to have a high school, agricultural school, and a daycare center. The supermarket we had passed on the way to the farm, as well as a hospital and polyclinic, are located in the nearby town and available to them. Medical services are free, of course.

There are plans for a collective dining room and a social center with its own movie facilities. Now they have a portable projector and screen, and films brought in from town. They subscribe to magazines and newspapers, have bought books, and intend to have a real library of their own. They also anticipate a supermarket with a variety of food and merchandise.

"But you can't expect to have all these things for just thirty adults and twenty children?"

"Oh, no," said one of them, as they all laughed, "we are only the pioneers of this collective farm. Our success will attract more people all the time. Remember, we are not doing this just for ourselves. We believe in the revolution and the future. Sometime in the not too distant future there will be hundreds here. We are already planning a dairy farm and may even raise hogs."

"Do you have private plots for vegetables and fruits?"

"Yes, but they are only for our own use; we do not intend to grow produce to sell at markets. We have other more important things to do."

We asked one last question: "How do you get along together? Isn't it difficult for people who have always lived and worked in the small family unit to work closely together with others?"

Elsa Rodríguez answered: "You forget another side of a farmer's character. He is more easygoing than city people and has a more relaxed approach to life. As for family, we consider we are now a larger family."

Then, with a smile, she said, "I suppose you know that Cuba grows the best coffee in the world. Well our's here is the best of the best. You must taste it before you leave."

16. Farming ain't the same

Olga had also arranged an interview for us with a national leader of ANAP, the farmers' organization. The interview took place in ANAP's headquarters in Havana, with Juan A. Santana Cruz, the head of its department on international relations.

At the outset of his remarks, Santana pointed out that while the movement of small farmers into co-ops was new, the idea was not. It was contained in the original Agrarian Reform Law (1959) that gave land to more than 200,000 peasant families. But until recently, it had been impossible to implement this concept. To speak of cooperatives to people whose families over generations had dreamed of owning their own land, was like speaking of communism. And at that time, even though peasants really knew nothing about communism, they had been misled into believing it was an unmitigated evil.

He illustrated this problem with an anecdote: In the early period of the revolutionary government, Fidel asked a peasant whom he met for the first time, "How do you like the agrarian reform?"

"I like it very much, Fidel," was the reply, "It's simply wonderful."

"And what do you think of the housing reform?"

"I like it very much Fidel, I like it very much." (This reform automatically made a tenant who had lived in a dwelling for twenty years, its owner).

And so it went, question after question, until Fidel asked, "And what do you think of Communism?"

"Oh, no," replied the peasant emphatically, "I don't like it; it's bad."

"So you see," said Santana, "the kind of problem we faced!"

He told us that at the First Congress of the Communist Party, in 1975, it was pointed out that private ownership of land was holding back greater farm production. This made it more difficult to bring electricity to all farms, particularly those in outlying and mountainous regions, or to make machinery available.

The Congress was followed by a period of experimentation. At the 6th ANAP Congress in 1980, the successful results of the first cooperative farm efforts were reported. Since then the movement toward co-ops has been quite rapid, "not as much in numbers," he added, "as in its effect. At present (the end of 1982), there are 1,402 farm co-ops in the country, representing 46% of all farm land. Of 190,000 small farmers, 58,000 are in co-ops; of these, 21% are women."

We interrupted to ask why such a low percentage of women. Santana mentioned a number of reasons: the exodus of young women from the countryside; the many who went to the university and from there into professions; the lack of daycare centers in many of the new co-ops; and that only now are the co-ops beginning to process their own produce, opening up new opportunities for women.

These answers did not seem to respond fully to the question, for most of the reasons affect men as well as women. Somewhat later, Santana referred to the fact that a considerable percentage of the older generation preferred to remain on their private plots. As women generally live longer than men, this may mean that there are considerably more women still on private plots. There may be a somewhat greater conservatism among these farm women. But these are only our conjectures.

Santana said that in September, 1982 there were 435 farm co-ops in sugar production; 228 in tobacco; 168 in cattle; and numerous others producing fruits and vegetables. "We are satisfied with both the number of co-ops and with the results obtained. All co-ops have done well, despite the diseases that hit sugar, tobacco, and hogs. Wherever a farm co-op has been established, production has increased from two- to four-fold."

New farm technology is constantly being introduced. Most sugarcane is now gathered by Cuban-made harvesters, each harvester replacing the labor of fifty workers. Thousands of tractors and trucks are in use. Last year alone, the farm co-ops received more than two million pesos worth of new machinery. Most co-ops are now constructing their own communities with electricity, refrigerators, TVs, washing machines, etc. Thus the co-ops are beginning to reduce the disparity between city and country life.

A number of new laws are now being discussed among co-op farmers, dealing with insurance, land resale, taxes and free markets. "Up to now, farmers paid no taxes to the state, despite being covered by social security, health care, etc. Now, because the co-ops are doing so well, they can contribute to meet the costs of the social benefits they receive. Co-op farmers have agreed to this principle."

One law is on crop insurance. Up to now, the state has covered such losses. For example, the tobacco mold that wiped out production for two years was covered by government grants. Now, two percent of farm income will go to insure crops and all co-op facilities. This insurance is not compulsory, but it is most important, for it ensures cooperatives against any form of catastrophe.

A law covering the free markets is also being drafted. This will try to guarantee better supplies to the consumer while stimulating farm production with greater profit incentives. Even though there is a charge for the market space used, the profits have been relatively high. In some cases, particularly in Havana, there has been some profiteering. Havana is special because of its high population density (about 2 million), a somewhat higher standard of living, and the more complex problems of getting supplies to the consumer. Because the character of the free market has sometimes been distorted in Havana, with even middlemen entering the scene, corrective measures are being drawn up. "Prices," said Santana, "will continue to be higher than in the rationed markets, but not as a market in which the sky is the limit."

We asked about the supply of manufactured goods to the countryside. Santana assured us that, generally speaking, the supermarkets and stores in the country have more to sell than those in Havana. There has been a conscious government policy to give more to the countryside. In the past, one could tell the difference between a farmer and a city person by what they wore. "But on the streets of Havana today, you can't tell who is visiting from the country or living in the city; they dress alike. While no one in Cuba has twenty pairs of shoes, neither is anyone without shoes."

17. Prisoners and justice

Prior to our leaving for Cuba, numerous articles had appeared in the daily press about the alleged mistreatment of political prisoners in Cuba. Particular attention was focused on one, Armando Valladares, released from a Cuban prison a short while before. He was being hailed as a brilliant 45-year-old poet and "a former student leader and ally of Mr. Castro." Valladares, it was said, had become paralyzed in prison due to mistreatment, and was confined to a wheel chair.

Suspecting that this was just another ruse in the concerted effort to sully the reputation of the Cuban Government, I nonetheless decided to see someone in Cuba's Justice Department for the facts. It turned out that the man I saw was Raúl Amaro, the President of Cuba's Supreme Court.

Chief Justice Amaro said that he knew of the campaign in the U.S. to besmirch Cuban justice and that it was not new; it had gone on for twenty-four years. He asserted that there are no political prisoners in Cuban prisons, only counterrevolutionaries, and that he would shortly explain the difference. "The most recent campaign is about Valladares. They say he's a poet, even a famous one. But no one in Cuba knows him as such. The only poem he ever wrote was one in prison called "From a Wheel Chair," as though he were paralyzed. He claims to have been a revolutionist and close to Fidel. All lies. He was a policeman during the Batista dictatorship and we have the documents to prove it. After the revolution, he was captured as a member of a counterrevolutionary gang, not because he criticized the government; no one goes to prison in Cuba for that. Valladares was involved in terrorist acts; he was caught with explosives in his possession. These are the facts. His claims of mistreatment and becoming paralyzed are also fiction. You will soon see for yourselves, now that he is out of Cuba."

I mentioned an article that had appeared in the *Miami News* on the day we left for Havana. It quoted a letter (allegedly smuggled out of a Cuban prison) claiming that 33 political prisoners were being kept in jail despite having served their full sentences. On this matter, too, Amaro said he had received many letters from the States. "But if a prisoner's sentence has been served, why should we keep him there? Many prisoners are freed long before the expiration of their sentences. Those who do not agree with the revolution can speak their minds, and to anyone. For us, this is more than a legal question; it is a moral one, a question of principle. During the guerrilla war, when revolutionists were being tortured, maimed and killed in cold blood, our treatment of prisoners was exemplary, as the whole world acknowledged."

Then the Chief Justice discussed a problem that they do have—that of *plantados*. "In every penal system," he explained, "there is work that prisoners must do. The work in our prisons is no different from that on the outside, and the salaries we pay prisoners are also the same. In this way they can learn skills, whether as machinists, plumbers, or carpenters, and with their wages pay for some costs, buy things in the commissary, or send money to their families. When they leave they can take with them whatever is left.

"This is important, because our prison system assumes the responsibility of finding a job for every person who is released.

"Counterrevolutionary prisoners have the same rights as other prisoners, but we do not pamper them or give them special privileges. Those who don't want to work, don't have to, but they cannot expect the same rights as those who do work. The *plantados* refuse to work, study, or participate in any activities; even refuse to wear prison garb. The name *plantados* comes from their planting themselves in this position and refusing to budge. They may think this will help them should they leave Cuba for some other country upon their release, but it certainly won't help them here. Apparently this is what is meant by our 'mistreating' them."

While it was impossible for us to pass judgment on Cuba's prison system or on some of the facts stated by the Chief Justice, I could, from personal experience, confirm his observation that usually prisoners have to perform some work. In Leavenworth Penitentiary, where I spent a number of years as a Communist (Smith Act) political prisoner, an inmate who refused to work landed in the hole. There were two kinds of work: in maintenance, for which a prisoner got no pay; and in industry, where the pay started at 12¢ an hour and peaked at the munificent wage of 48¢ an hour. I spent most of my prison years working in prison industry. If Cuba pays its prisoners the same wages as they would receive on the outside, that indeed is something we could learn from. Nor did those of us who were political prisoners in the U.S. ask for special privileges or separate treatment, only not to be treated worse than ordinary prisoners. I said something to this effect to the Chief Justice. I also said that judging by what we now know of the nefarious activities of the CIA all over the world, and of its specific attempts to cause chaos in Cuba and to assassinate its leaders, it is not surprising that there are a considerable number of counterrevolutionary prisoners.

We then inquired about the penal code adopted in 1979. We were informed that some acts previously considered criminal were deleted. He gave two examples; prostitution, and the landing of foreign planes or boats by accident. Prostitution, he pointed out, is a social problem. When conditions change it is eliminated, as it has been in Cuba.

The length of sentences was also reduced. Ways of treating juvenile crime were changed, with far less punishment for those under twenty years of age than those older. A special code on juvenile delinquency is being prepared which will completely remove such cases from criminal courts to a special agency of the educational system.

We asked how great was the problem of juvenile delinquency. We were told it is very low. "We do not have juvenile gangs such as you have in the States, nor bank robbers. Our juvenile crimes are usually committed by single individuals, rarely by two or three operating together. They consist mainly of petty acts directed against property, not people. As you can see," he said with a broad grin, "our delinquency is also underdeveloped."

There are also what Cubans call "economic crimes," involving theft, graft or corruption. (Helen and I had noticed one aspect of this when a Cuban friend in whose car we were riding carefully removed the windshield wipers before parking for the night.) Cuba has few homicides and these are usually the result of family quarrels. In addition to prostitution, drug traffic and gambling have also been eliminated. Cuba, we were proudly told, has one of the lowest crime rates in the world. "A main reason for this is that we have no unemployment."

The Cuban Government is particularly incensed at Reagan's charge of drug trading. It points to its record of systematically combatting international drug traffic with the arrest of hundreds whose boats or planes carrying drugs were caught in Cuban territorial waters or airspace. It has demanded that the U.S. Government provide even a scintilla of evidence to back up its outrageous charges.

Chief Justice Amaro also told us that prison conditions were constantly improving, with more and better cultural facilities. "The purpose of prisons is to rehabilitate people, not to punish them. We must have conditions, therefore, that make it possible. Yes, we enforce discipline, but nothing is done to humiliate or denigrate, or to put a person under undue pressures. To do otherwise makes no sense. It would defeat our purpose. We do not want these people to leave prison as enemies of society; our purpose is their rehabilitation."

Then he spoke of the judicial system as a whole. Until 1974, there were revolutionary courts, military courts, labor courts and common-criminal courts. Each had its own jurisdiction. In 1974, the system was unified and new approaches were introduced. One very important change was in the system of lay judges. Another, all judges are now elected, even the President of the Supreme Court. (Lay judges, as we have seen, are elected by the Municipal Assemblies; the President, Vice-President and Associate Justices of the Supreme Court are elected by the National Assembly.) There is also a labor code to enforce, under which workers have the right to sue enterprises for any breach of labor laws.

Each lower court has fifteen lay judges who sit for two months each (three judges are alternates). Lay judges can be reelected, but the objective is to have considerable turnover so that more people can directly experience the judicial process. As we mentioned earlier, they attend courses to acquire a legal basis for their judgments.

"We have a problem," the Chief Justice told us, "an insufficiency of lawyers. There are only four law schools in Cuba. During the early years of the revolution, there was a rejection of legalisms so that no one wanted to study law, not even international law so important for world commerce."

Then, in response to further questions, he told us about the appeal procedure and the Supreme Court. Every person found guilty in a lower court has the right to appeal the conviction or sentence. The appeal procedure is simple. It requires a letter to the next higher court stating disagreement with the results of the trial, and why. The provincial court must respond within two days and a hearing must be held within twenty days. At this level the plaintiff must be represented by an attorney, either of his own selection or by court appointment should he so desire; in either case, free of charge. An appeal to the Supreme Court takes longer, usually from two to three months.

Those convicted of crimes can be sentenced to prison terms, house arrest, periodic reports to the court, or having one's workplace or a mass organization take responsibility for his or her conduct. But a person who has been proven to be a menace to society, goes to prison.

"We don't claim all is perfect," the Chief Justice said. "We know we still have unsolved problems, but the important thing is recognizing them so that we can do something about them. Everyone here has a right to complain, or criticize even the highest court of the land. I receive scores of letters every day, and I am required to answer each and every one of them."

18. Revolution in education

C uba's remarkable achievement in educating its people is now universally recognized, but we had no idea how profound the changes had been since our last visit. In our talk with Cuba's Ministry of Education, its Deputy Director, Fernando García (not to be confused with our young friend of the same name), explained something of this process to us.

We were first reminded of the immense changes since the revolution. In 1958, 56% of children 6 to 12 years old were in school; today, school attendance for this age group is universal and compulsory. The country is now making schooling for those from 13 to 16 years old compulsory. This leap in schooling has occurred during the greatest "baby boom" in Cuban history. In 1970, Cuba's population was eight million; today, it is ten million. This increase was induced, it is believed, partly by the general feeling of security and optimism which followed the revolutionary victory, as well as better health care.

Hence today, 3.5 million children and youth, or 35% of Cuba's total population, are in school. (This compares with but 23% in the U.S.) The huge financial burden education imposes on Cuba's economy is self-evident. Yet, as in respect to health expenditures, Cuba considers it an essential investment for the future.

Once having made a breakthrough in mass education, Cuba's leaders—pedagogical as well as political—turned their main attention to the character and quality of education. As García put it, "To fully change a system requires more than a change in one of its elements; it requires a change in all of them. This is the problem we faced in the early 1970s."

To grapple with this problem, a national educational conference was convened in 1971. It concluded that a virtual revolution was needed in the approach to education. After a considerable period of further intensive probing, two major changes were decided upon. First, to combine study and work as a basic principle guiding *all* education; second, to restructure the educational system by introducing a series of subsystems into it, beginning with the daycare centers and pre-primary school training.

The concept of integrally relating study and work is not new. It was a basic view held by both Karl Marx and Jose Martí. They saw it as an essential means to end the age-old dichotomy between mental and physical labor, in which a few are ordained the thinkers and the great mass of people are the producers. Only a living link between thinking and doing could close the gap which had developed in class society between theory and practice, schools and life, teaching and producing.

Already in 1959, Fidel had posed the problem. He said that it is not enough to teach children to read and write; they must also know about work and the need to serve others. One can never fully comprehend reality, he stressed, without experiencing the sweat of physical labor.

Some years later, Fidel said that those who perform only physical labor are brutalized and deformed by it, but that also brutalized and deformed are those who perform only intellectual labor. A truly human society, he reasoned, is one in which everyone participates in both.

This principle was already being applied in boarding schools when we visited Cuba in 1969. Now, it is being applied to all education.

Combining study with work begins early. Even in kindergarten and in elementary school, children are given tasks and responsibilities; through the tending of school gardens, they learn something about how vegetables, fruits and flowers grow. In secondary school, children actually work 45 days a year in a program known as "school *to* the countryside." Taking part in this program requires parental agreement.

Edmundo and Cari Suárez are a couple with two boys, Ricardo and Eduardo. When we visited their home in Havana, Riqui, fourteen and in secondary school, was out of the city doing his 45-day stint in the country. As he returned to the city on weekends, we made arrangements to see him one Sunday. We saw a tired, yet happy youngster. He had stayed up late the night before, dancing, and then took a bus ride to the city. His countryside job was picking coffee beans and he had thorn cuts on his hands to prove it. He wore these as proudly as a soldier with combat medals. For him, it was a great adventure as well as a learning experience. He now had a new kind of respect for farm people who did this work all the time. He now knew the arduous labor required to bring coffee to his family's table, and had a greater respect for the skills involved. He had also gotten a deeper view of the role of labor in human society.

Another variant of the link between study and labor is the "school *in* the countryside." This is a boarding school of young people from the same general community. They live, study and work together. We visited the Bárbaro Alvarez Ramirez Boarding School in Cienfuegos Province. As at the mill earlier, this school was named for another young man who had lived and worked here and had volunteered to go to Angola where he was killed at age twenty-one. A large sign with his photo told of his life and heroism.

This is a senior high school with students in the 10th, 11th and 12th grades. It is an honor to go to a boarding school and the students come with higher than average grades. Of 530 students, 262 were female. There were 42 teachers. The school is run by a council on which sit a representative of the student body, the trade union, and the Young Communist League.

On five days a week, four hours are devoted each morning to classroom courses, and three hours in the afternoon to work. This is field work, mainly that of caring for citrus trees and picking the fruit. In the evening there is study and recreation. On weekends the students go home, with free transportation both ways.

There is a relatively new and rapidly growing citrus industry in Cuba. When we were there previously, it was largely concentrated on the Isle of Youth (formerly the Isle of Pines). Now it is spread all over Cuba. When we drove from Havana to Cienfuegos, we saw mile after mile of newly-planted citrus trees. We were told that high school students make up a considerable proportion of the work-force that tends these groves.

We also visited what was described as "the most important polytechnical institute in Cuba." It is located in Havana's University City and is named for a university student who had been murdered during the Batista dictatorship, José Antonio Echeverría.

This institute is large and most impressive. It consists of forty-three buildings for classrooms, laboratories, libraries, auditoriums, administrative offices, dormitories and sports facilities. It has 15,000 students, nearly 3,000 of whom live in the dormitories. There are ten faculties and forty-eight teaching departments. The institute publishes seven prestigious scientific journals, and its faculties cover nearly all branches of technology and engineering, including automatic control systems, computerization and solar energy.

Here too, study and work are organically linked. The institute plays a direct role in helping industries and enterprises solve difficult engineering and technological problems. Students spend from six to eight weeks a year working at such enterprises. Thus, general theoretical knowledge is bolstered by important practical experience.

THE DIVISION of general education into specific subsystems begins with preschool training. A child can be admitted to a daycare center as early as 45 days after birth. Why so young? "Because," said García, "we have determined scientifically that the human personality begins to develop at an extremely young age. Games are played in the daycare centers that help develop the child's mind and imagination. It is also important for the working mother, who otherwise would be tied down at home. When we first started these centers in 1961, reactionaries spread the word that we were taking children from their parents, even sending them to the Soviet Union and other such nonsense. Now parents clamor to get their children into the centers for, unfortunately, we still do not have as many as we need. Parental request is, of course, a requirement for a child's entry." Preschool education is seen as laying the foundation for the future development of the child and its preparation for kindergarten at age five.

Elementary school is divided into two age cycles: the 1st through 3rd grade and the 4th through 6th grade. The first cycle concentrates on language and arithmetic. It also helps inculcate habits of study and the ability to do independent thinking and work. During this cycle the children have just one teacher who advances with them to the end of the 3rd grade. This enables greater familiarity with the learning progress of each child and individualized attention to those who need it. The second cycle continues the child's development, but different subjects are taught by different teachers.

Secondary education is in like manner divided into two cycles: the lower one, comparable with our junior high schools, covers 7th, 8th and 9th grades. The upper cycle, corresponding to our senior high school and considered to be pre-university, goes through the 12th grade. From elementary school through high school, the ratio of teacher to students is 1 to 13. In the United States it is 1 to 25, and in some places 1 to 30 or even 40.

Cuba has developed complex subsystems of specialized education, including schools for various types of physical or mental impairment. Another subsystem comprises vocational and technological schools. A child finishing 9th grade can choose to enroll in a 1- to 2-year school for skilled workers, or in a 3- to 4-year school for middle-level technicians.

There are many other educational subsystems, covering pedagogy, social science, Cuban and world literature, all forms of art and culture, etc. In the general educational courses from grade 1 through grade 12, about 40 percent of the time is allocated to science, a few percent less to the humanities, and the rest is divided between esthetics, work education, electives, etc. One other subsystem is considered to be of great importance, that of adult education.

"Every student a worker and every worker a student," is a popular slogan in Cuba. The emphasis is placed on education as a lifelong process, a socialist way of life. Most of the people we talked to, irrespective of age, kind of work engaged in, or educational level, were taking courses in one subject or another, The main task of this subdivision is to enable workers to continue acquiring knowledge and culture. A worker who wishes to leave a job for full-time schooling is encouraged to do so and receives half of his or her average on-job earnings while in school. The education itself, including textbooks, is totally free, as it is for all students in Cuba.

In addition to formal courses, Cuba's educational system encourages students to organize informal "interest circles." There are more than 20,000 scientific-technological interest circles with more than 300,000 participants. There are also circles on sports, literature, and a mass amateur art movement with its own subdivisions of music, drama, dance, plastic arts and choral groups. Over 100,000 amateur art groups exist.

Municipal, provincial and national amateur art festivals are held regularly, and visits are organized to museums, art galleries, and historic monuments. In every educational institution there are literary workshops, plastic arts workshops and film discusson groups.

We saw something of this when we spent a day at Varadero where the international festival of the New Song Movement was being held. For a full week, 40,000 people jammed a huge outdoor amphitheater each night to listen to the songs and music of Cuba, Latin America, the United States, and other countries. It was an exuberant, joyous, youthful crowd, with a reciprocal interaction between audience and performers. When we left at 1:00 a.m., the festivities were still going strong.

Before saying goodbye at the Ministry of Education, we asked a last question: "What do you consider to be your main problem at this time?" The answer came in one word: "Quality." Then García explained: "Our educational system is so young and new that often it is difficult to tell who in the classroom is the teacher; they are all of approximately the same age. Yes, we have achieved a great deal, but we need a still higher quality in our teaching and our work."

19. The young generation

Y outh played an important role in the Cuban Revolution from its inception. The guerrilla army that fought the Batista dictatorship was mostly composed of youth, both workers and students. When we visited Cuba in 1969 and 1970 we were impressed by the number of young people in posts of responsibility. This followed a long tradition of revolutionary youth movement and activity. The present prominent Federation of University Students dates back more than a half century and was formed by Julio Mella, a martyr of the struggle against the Machado dictatorship, and a founder of the earlier Communist Party.

The tradition continues. Even twenty-five years after its victory, the Cuban Revolution exudes a youthful spirit and style; the young generation is actively involved in all aspects of social life.

The present Cuban youth movement is as colorful and varied as is the island's flora. It tries to respond to all the interests of youth and to take into account inevitable generational differences in experience and perception. The stress is on study, work and struggle, with all three considered essential and integral to life. Artistic and cultural forms, and particularly modern music, are interwoven into nearly everything.

Of the many youth organizations that exist, the Young Communist League is by far the most important. It has a half million members, yet only those who actively support the revolution and socialism can join. About half of its members are workers, a fourth are students, the rest professional or farm youth. Its age range is from fourteen years to thirty, with half of its members under twenty-four; forty percent are female.

In discussing the youth movement with Renie Díaz, (a young man in his late twenties and a national leader of the YCL) we got a picture of its many activities. Díaz began by telling us about the YCL's responsibility for guiding the children's organization, the José Martí Young Pioneers. This is a movement of two million children age six to thirteen. It is divided into two divisions; children from first to fourth grade and those from fifth to ninth grade. A major objective of work with the younger age group is to help establish a close bond between school and home. A second objective, Díaz said, is to stimulate the child's natural inquisitiveness, and desire to learn. "We do not want our children to be all alike. We want them to develop their own individual aptitudes and personalities, but," he added, "as a part of collective life, not as individualists."

The YCL also helped form and actively supports the mass organization of high school students of 300,000 members, which represents the students on school administrative councils "and sometimes opposes the policies of school authorities."

A third student organization is the previously mentioned Federation of University Students. It has 90,000 members and is strongly internationalist in outlook. While its main stress is on study, its members volunteer to go wherever there is need for teachers, nurses, doctors, engineers or farm specialists in countries of Latin America, Africa or Asia.

The YCL is the patron saint to a host of other cultural and special interest movements. The New Song Movement, whose festival we attended, is one of them. It combines folk and modern music, with lyrics frequently on social themes. It has about 2,000 members and is restricted to those with skills as musicians, composers, singers or arrangers.

There is also a brigade movement of young writers which unites about 4,000 writers and poets. An organization of art school graduates provides instructors for the thousands of amateur art groups around the country. Another important brigade movement is that of young technicians. Many new inventions and technological innovations have come from its ranks. There is also an important brigade movement of young farmers which fills the role of a living link between the private farmers and those in the new cooperatives.

After listening to Díaz explain the complexity of youth organizations and activities, we asked a question we had previously put to other Cubans. What, we wanted to know, explained the exodus from Cuba of thousands of young people during the Mariel episode in the summer of 1980.

Díaz replied that he understood why we asked this question, but that what happened at Mariel does not reflect the attitude of the great majority of young people to the revolution and socialism. He gave an example. When a call was issued for 2,000 teacher volunteers to go to Nicaragua to help in its literacy campaign, more than 57,000 young teachers applied. "This is the kind of revolutionary spirit we find everywhere," he said, "yet some visitors who come here from capitalist countries have idealized notions of what to expect. In one instance visitors were shocked when they saw a street brawl. They asked, 'How can this happen in a socialist country?' as if the revolution had turned everyone into an angel.

"Other visitors were surprised when someone told them that some husbands are still jealous of their wives and resent their leaving home unescorted. But this is a country in transition, with the old and the new in constant battle. We do not want people to think that everything is perfect, but neither do we want them to draw the conclusion that everything is wrong just because some things are still wrong."

Then, reminding himself of still another example, Díaz continued, "We've even had visitors from extremely poor countries in Latin America, where most people are half-starved and half-naked, express surprise that our store windows did not display as much merchandise as those in their countries. They didn't seem to realize that if we gave less of our national income to the people, our stores, too, would be overstocked with merchandise."

Cuba, he reminded us, is an island, but not isolated from the rest of the world and certainly not from the influences of the U.S. and its "consumer society." "Remember, we can easily tune in on radio stations in Miami, Key West or elsewhere, and hear advertisements for this or that gadget. Sure, young people here often want things that others have, and sometimes they may forget that they have things others do not. We will never have twenty different brands of toothpaste, for example, and will not compete on that level. But we are more than ready to compete when it comes to free education, free culture, free health care, jobs and opportunities for all, and a free atmosphere in which young people can speak their minds without fear of any kind."

"Did the large number of visits from Cubans living in the States create some problems in this respect?" we asked.

"Yes, of course," was his reply. "They brought with them things that are still lacking or scarce here and tales about how good life has been for them, although some of them gasped in surprise when they saw the social services we have here and the other changes wrought by the revolution. But whatever the negative effects, we do not want to close our doors to visitors, whether Cubans or others. We have nothing to hide and a great deal to be proud of. It is the Reagan government, apparently, which is afraid to let people see our country for themselves."

In asking others about those who left Cuba, we got a variety of responses. One person said that beneficiaries of the old regime often pass on to their children their own negative attitudes. Others pointed to the fact that many of those who left were school drop-outs; that some sought escape from too-early marriages; and that while there was a great deal of activity centered around educational institutions, insufficient attention is given to organizing neighbor-hood youth activities. One person told us that he thought many left "just for the sake of adventure," while others said that every society has some malcontents and Cuba is no exception.

Probably the most important reason was given by Fidel when he said that despite all that the revolution had given to the people, life in Cuba was still hard and that the present generation must still make sacrifices for those to come. Building a socialist society, he emphasized, is a voluntary act; those who do not want to participate in it are free to leave.

The people we spoke to were agreed on one thing: that the Mariel episode was not symptomatic of youth's attitude toward the revolu-tion, even though it was indicative of some problems. The young generation on the whole, we were assured, is even more revolution-ary than the older one.

20. Being color blind

Coming from a country where racial prejudice and discrimination are endemic, we found it hard to believe that things were totally different in Cuba. After all, Cuba, too, had a large black population, a heritage of slavery, and a history of discrimination.

We asked Nancy Echeverría, our young black interpreter, "Are there really no racial problems in Cuba?"

"I understand why it is so difficult for someone coming from the United States to understand," she answered, "but there is no racial problem here because there is no discrimination here. Black people are equal, enjoying all rights and opportunities. Of course, here and there you can still find a bigoted person, but these are fast disappearing and no one dares advocate or practice discrimination."

Later, we met with an old friend of my youth, Severo Aguirre del Cristo. He was the leader of the Cuban Communist youth organization in the 1930s when I was active in the Young Communist League in the States. He is black, for many years the Cuban Ambassador to the Soviet Union, presently a member of the Central Committee of Cuba's Communist Party, on the government's Council of State, and the President of *El Movimiento Cubano por la Paz y la Soberanía de los Pueblos,* Cuba's important peace and international solidarity movement.

We embraced, reminisced about old times, exchanged information about our families, discussed the grave international situation and the danger of nuclear war, and then I asked him the same question I had formerly asked Nancy. "Take my word for it, Gil," he replied, "we have abolished racial discrimination forever. Of course, it was never the same here as in the U.S., but sufficiently similar. Before our revolution, black Cubans suffered the most unemployment, the lowest wages and the least education."

Then he spoke in a more personal vein. "During the Batista dictatorship, I functioned in the Party's underground leadership with a special responsibility for work among peasants. As you know, a large percentage of black Cubans were on the land, particularly in Oriente Province. When I think back about conditions then and the immense changes our revolution wrought, I become highly emotional. Yesterday, there was intense poverty and illiteracy; today, peasant sons and daughters get scholarships and graduate from universities as agricultural scientists, doctors, engineers and teachers. When I see the difference in the way our peasants live today, I realize once again how truly liberating was our revolution. Let me give you one little example. Today, peasant women give birth in hospitals. Can you appreciate what that means? But more. How do we solve the problem of pregnant women who live some distance from a hospital? There are now special homes adjacent to hospitals where pregnant women can come some time prior to the expected date of birth, be taken care of without charge of any kind, and then enter the hospital as soon as they feel the first labor pains."

Returning to the question I had asked, Aguirre added, "Yes, we still have people with prejudice, but no one is permitted to discriminate. You can see the results in education, in the extremely large and growing number of black teachers."

Thinking about this, I realized why he had placed emphasis on education. Giving people equal rights does not automatically guarantee them *full* equality, especially if there is still inequality in the level of education, training and experience. This explains why the preponderance of scholarships went to the children and youth of the very poorest families, especially from the countryside. It enables them to make up in double-quick time for the immense lag imposed upon them by discrimination and poverty. It was affirmative action, Cuban style.

Aguirre had said that the pre-revolutionary situation in Cuba was "sufficiently similar" to that in the States, but not the same. The differences are important.

In the first place, the *majority* of Cubans are of both Spanish *and* African descent. A person is called black in Cuba if either all, or nearly all his lineage is African. This is different from the U.S., where anyone with even the slightest trace of African heritage is considered to be Black, even if the color of their skin is more light than dark. In other words, racial prejudice and discrimination in the United States has been and remains far more pervasive than formerly existed in Cuba.

There is also an important historic factor to be considered. All working people in the United States suffer one or another degree of capitalist exploitation, but only the racial minorities—Afro-American, Native American Indian, Hispanic and Asian peoples—suffer discrimination and oppression as peoples. In Cuba, on the other hand, the entire nation, irrespective of skin color, suffered from intense national oppression. In the U.S., we won national independence and sovereignty through the revolution of 1776. The Cuban nation, however, was oppressed by Spanish colonial rule up to the end of the 19th century, and then, having won independence by a long, drawn-out and heroic people's war, was subjugated once again, this time by U.S. imperialist domination. Only the Castro-led revolution brought Cuba complete sovereignty.

The recognition of common identity as an oppressed nation dictated the need for interracial unity in the war against Spain and later against the Batista dictatorship as the oppressive arm of Washington and Wall Street.

Cuba's arduous struggle against Spanish rule brought to the fore two of its greatest leaders—Jose Martí, the brilliant revolutionary intellectual, and Antonio Maceo, the great military strategist. Both Martí, white, and Maceo, black, understood the crucial importance of white-black unity. Martí wrote to Maceo in 1882: "There can be no political solution of the Cuban problem without a social solution. And this solution can only be obtained with the love and mutual respect of the one race for the other."

When in that same period, Juan Gualberto Gómez, a prominent black Cuban leader, believed it was necessary to establish a separate organization of blacks and mulattoes in the revolutionary struggle, Maceo disagreed. He argued that this "would play into the hands of the enemies of the revolution." The struggle could only succeed, he was convinced, "through the unity of Negro and white Cubans." The Spanish authorities "were especially upset by the fact that leading white Cubans looked up to the Negro revolutionist [Maceo] as a logical leader in the struggle to liberate the island."*

Likewise in the struggle against the Batista dictatorship, Oriente Province and its main city, Santiago de Cuba, with large black majorities, were the heart and soul of the revolution, notwithstanding the fact that Batista was mulatto.

These are important historic factors that helped make the path toward racial equality easier, but the decisive element was the determination of the revolutionary regime to abolish every form of discrimination with stern enforcement.

Everywhere we went we saw black and white Cubans together at complete ease with one another; in schools, institutions, neighborhoods, the fishing complex in Cienfuegos, the New Song Festival at Varadero, in hotels, restaurants and the little Bodegita bar that Ernest Hemingway made famous (which is still a favorite spot for authors, journalists and artists). Helen and I made note of this to one another, but said nothing to Cubans, for it seemed as though we alone were color conscious and everyone else, color blind. For them, it was the most natural thing in the world, and so it is, for the most unnatural is the prejudice of judging people by the pigmentation of their skins. We felt envious of the Cubans for grasping this simple truth.

*All quotations from Phillip S. Foner's *A History of Cuba,* Volume II, International Publishers, NYC, pp 313-14, 319.

21. The Communist Party

Cuba has but one political party, the Communist Party. To most people in our country this is self-evident proof that there is no democracy in Cuba. But democracy is not determined by the number of parties a country has but whether government truly is of, by and for the people. In this sense, democracy is very much alive and well in Cuba.

The Cuban people freely elect their own representatives by secret ballot, and the limited wealth of this small, developing island is more equally and fairly divided among its people than in our own extremely rich country, where monopoly capital is euphemistically called "free enterprise," where a corporate oligarchy lives in obscene gluttony while millions are jobless and tens of millions live in abject and humiliating poverty.

A decade ago the president of the United Mine Workers Union told his membership, "We have only one political party in this country—the Money Party; and it has two branches, the Republican and the Democratic branch."

Cuba's Communist Party is not a "Money Party." It is a workers' and people's party. Nor is it an electoral party. It runs no candidates and endorses none. If this seems strange to some, they should look back at our own country's history. At the time of the founding of our republic, the revolutionary fathers did not foresee the rise of sharply contending political parties. They thought that candidates could be elected to office on their personal records and merits. In the first elections for the Presidency, the candidate with the highest vote in the Electoral College became the President; the one with the next highest, the Vice-President. When the Federalist and Republican Parties (not to be confused with that of today) came on the scene, the U.S. Constitution was amended in 1804 to make it possible for Presidential and Vice-Presidential candidates to run on the same ticket.

But if Cuba's Communist Party is not an electoral party, why is it needed and what is its role? These questions go to the heart of what the Cuban Revolution is all about and what it aims to attain. A vast social revolution is taking place in Cuba, the objective of which is the total transformation of society into a classless one, without either rulers or ruled.

This could not be accomplished by the single act of taking power, as indispensable as that was. It can only be achieved by a long period of ongoing revolutionary changes in both the material conditions of life and in the thinking of people. For class divisions in society have existed for thousands of years and the mentality of the past had accepted upper and lower classes as the natural order of things, even as God-given.

To change the thinking of people is not only an ideological process, as decisive as that is. It also requires changing material reality, to show in life that a new kind of society is not only possible, but is actually being built. In turn, this entails for a country as economically underdeveloped as Cuba a difficult and prolonged struggle for economic development. Without it there can be no substantial improvement in the material and cultural life of the people, and therefore no way to overcome existing income disparities, personal greed, and the craving for material possessions as the prime goal in life. This struggle for economic development must be won despite a lack of natural resources, particularly energy, and in the face of the open hostility and threats of the world's largest and mightiest imperialist power, only a figurative stone's throw away.

Cuba's Communist Party sees its role as that of a moral, ideological and organizational motive force propelling the revolution onward despite all difficulties and obstacles, while guaranteeing the defense of the revolution against the never-ending danger of imperialist attack. It frankly affirms that there is working-class rule in Cuba, and contrasts this with the dictatorship of big capital that exists in every capitalist country irrespective of the form of government. In capitalist states, constitutional law upholds and defends the system of private ownership of the productive facilities and natural resources; in Cuba, law defends and sustains the system of public, collective ownership.

Not everyone can be a member of Cuba's Marxist-Leninist Party. They must be worthy of that honor. Before an applicant is accepted, fellow workers and neighbors are consulted. Should they lack confidence in that person, their views are seriously taken into account. Fidel has repeatedly stressed that the people judge the Party by the quality of its members and leaders. These must be exemplary workers and exemplary human beings; the first in line to serve, the last on the receiving end.

The CP sees as its cardinal role that of raising the socialist consciousness of the people, of publicly exposing all weaknesses and shortcomings in the battle for economic development, and of stimulating the people's initiative and the role of the mass organizations. When we visited the large fishing complex in Cienfuegos, we saw a huge banner strung across the main entrance. It read, *La fueza del partido radica en su vinculación estrecha con las masas* — "The strength of the party lies in its close ties with the masses." This slogan, or a variation of it, was everywhere.

Extremely impressive to us was the careful way in which the Party avoids interfering with the independence of the mass organizations, particularly the trade unions. A key resolution adopted at the First Congress of the Party in 1975, warned its local organizations and members against trying to impose their own standards on the mass organizations, or meddling in their affairs or usurping their roles. When differences arise, it was urged that these be resolved by patient reasoning "in an atmosphere of fraternal discussion"; never by undermining the authority of the organization's leadership. If no Party member is on the executive committee of a local union or similar organization with which some differences have arisen, it is suggested that permission be asked for a Party member to attend a meeting to present its point of view.

There was a Communist organization in Cuba dating back to the 1920s, founded by Julio Mella, also a founder of the first revolutionary student organization. A brilliant Marxist and popular leader,

Mella was felled by an assassin's bullet at the order of the Machado dictatorship then in power.

The Cuban C.P. today is the result of a 1962 amalgam of the best of the two main revolutionary socialist currents, the July 26th Movement that conducted the heroic armed struggle against the Batista regime, and the older Communist movement with its deep roots in the working class. From the outset, the leader of the revolution, Fidel Castro, became the leader of the united party.

History is not made by the deeds of great men, but as Marx noted, the quality of those at the head of a movement at a given time is an important, often decisive, factor in the outcome of the struggle. Cuba is indeed fortunate, therefore, in having Fidel as its outstanding leader. He is Cuba's most popular and beloved personality, adored by the people as one of their own, to whom they can always raise their questions and problems. He is also a great mass educator, explaining the most complicated issues to the Cuban people in a simple, human language they can understand. He is especially a man with great vision and foresight, and confidence in the Cuban people. He is a firm Marxist-Leninist, who applies theory in a creative way to the specific Cuban conditions. While Cuban to his very core, he is also an internationalist in all his thinking, never viewing the problems of Cuba as separate and apart from those of humanity as a whole; he imbues the Cuban people with the spirit and ideals of working-class internationalism. He has said that Cuba will never be satisfied with plenty for itself if other peoples are hungry.

Nor has Castro ever permitted others to place him on a pedestal as the all-knowing fount of wisdom. On the contrary, we were present in the Plaza of the Revolution on July 26, 1970, when Fidel delivered a slashing criticism of the serious errors in economic policy that had been made, and assumed personal responsibility for them. A few days later we spoke to a worker in a factory and asked what the response to Fidel's admissions had been. The answer was: "Once again we know that our leadership will never lie to us." People know that every human being makes mistakes and respect those who admit them.

Of course, when such a leader arises, one who is not glued to a desk but out among the people, participating in every major campaign and responding to every emergency, there is always the

danger of decisions being made on-the-spot rather than by collective consultation. I asked Carlos Rafael Rodriguez about this when
we talked near the end of this visit. He assured me that there was
genuine collective leadership at all levels of the Party and government. I asked him about the danger of bureaucracy, pointing out
that the lofty principles and objectives of a movement can easily
become endangered by bureaucratic encrustment. He said that this
was very well understood by Cuban leaders and first of all by Fidel,
who is the most sensitive of all to any signs of corruption and
bureaucracy. A regional Party leader had said to us earlier, "Wherever there is corruption you will find bureaucracy, and wherever
there is bureaucracy you will find some forms of corruption."

When corruption even of a petty kind began to rear its head
shortly after the opening of the first free markets, Castro scathingly
denounced this to the entire nation, calling for measures to halt it.
At the 1st Congress of the Cuban CP, bureaucracy was condemned
in the sharpest language as the vice of the past most difficult to
eradicate; this was spelled out with numerous examples.

Acknowledging the past errors of romanticism, as in the failure
to understand the importance of material incentives as a means of
getting people to produce more, Castro has not forgotten the
decisive role of moral questions in the molding of a generation
dedicated to the building of a communist society. Speaking to the
4th Congress of the Cuban YCL on April 4, 1982, he told the youth
that by working better and harder more wealth is created from
which people can earn more for themselves, but that earning more
for oneself can never be the main objective of those who want to
attain the lofty goal of communism. He urged youth to be always
ready to work and sacrifice for the good of all.

This idealism and morality with which Fidel is identified in
everything he says or does is a powerful inspiring force helping a
new generation to keep its eyes, despite all present difficulties, on
the building of a truly human society.

22. Of blue sky and red fish

I t is quite understandable that the U.S. Government, beholden as it is and has been to serving the interests of U.S. monopoly capitalism at home and abroad, should look with animosity upon countries that take the socialist path. This is reason enough for its enmity toward the new Cuba. It does not, however, explain the pathological hatred of Cuba.

After all, in today's world there are many countries at various stages of socialist development. The U.S. has found it expedient and even profitable to establish diplomatic and commercial relations with nearly all of them. At times, it has even found it advisable to cooperate with a socialist country without giving up its general hostility to socialism as a competitive socioeconomic system. Its longest and greatest antagonism has been toward the Soviet Union, which it sees as the great world power standing in the way of U.S. world supremacy.

Why, however, the intensely irrational hatred of tiny Cuba? Why the refusal to grant it recognition, the cruel economic blockade maintained against it, and the many frenetic efforts to undermine and topple the Castro government? These actions cannot be explained solely by Cuba's socialist system or by its friendship with the Soviet Union, for they predate both Cuba's acceptance of socialism as a goal as well as its close ties with the Soviet Union.

The roots of U.S. intransigence to Cuba are imbedded in their historic relationship. Nearly from the outset of our republic, and particularly in the era of its greatest continental expansion, covetous eyes were cast on Cuba as a choice island to be annexed sooner or later by the U.S., just as was done to Puerto Rico after the war with Spain.

In 1895, for example, an important Wall Street figure wrote, "It makes the water come to my mouth when I think of the state of Cuba as one in our family." Another Wall Street spokesman had an even more voracious appetite. "Canada will come in time; Mexico will follow Texas and California, and drop into her niche under the stars and stripes. *But we want Cuba now.*" (Philip Foner, *A History of Cuba, Vol. II,* International Publishers, N.Y., 1963, p. 345.)

However, when the war against Spain was over, the U.S. corporations found Cuba too tough a morsel to swallow whole. They set out to devour it piecemeal, and first of all to establish the right to intervene, militarily if need be, in Cuba's internal affairs. The Platt Amendment to a military appropriation bill, asserting this right, was adopted by Congress in 1901. It was then incorporated into a formal treaty with Cuba. Five years later, in 1906, President Theodore Roosevelt made use of that right by sending U.S. troops into Cuba

In this way, the U.S. accepted Cuba's right to self-rule, as long as Cuba accepted the U.S. right to determine its policies and government. By the time the humiliating Platt Amendment was revoked in 1934, U.S. corporations had established complete control over the island.

From this historic imperialist view, the Cuban people had no right to overthrow the brutal Batista dictatorship which had ruled with U.S. aid and in U.S. corporate interests. The Cuban people, however, thought otherwise. They were determined to be independent, equal and sovereign, at long last.

This was treason in the eyes of the U.S. ruling class and called for aggressive counter measures. Hence the venemous hostility, the Bay of Pigs invasion, the economic blockade, the plots to murder Castro and other Cuban leaders, the refusal to establish diplomatic relations with Cuba, and the ridiculous charge that Cuba is the source of the seething unrest in Central America when hunger, exploitation and oppression are the real causes.

The most shocking and immoral of all the many crimes committed against Cuba by the U.S. is the use of biological warfare. Fidel Castro spoke of this when he addressed the 68th World Inter-Parliamentary Conference on September 15, 1981, in the presence of a number of members of the U.S. Congress:

> In less than three years time, five serious plagues and epidemics have scourged our land and—what is even worse—our population; swine fever, tobacco blue mold, sugar cane rust, hemorrhagic dengue and lastly, hemorrhagic conjunctivitis. . . . And in each case they appeared without logical explanation.

The dengue fever epidemic cost Cuba 156 lives including those of 99 children. According to Castro, this epidemic appeared suddenly, when no similar outbreak had occurred elsewhere. A group of Cuban scientists, with the help of foreign specialists, concluded that the virus had been deliberately introduced into Cuba. At the time this epidemic broke out in Cuba, no country with which it had relations and no incoming Cubans or foreigners from any part of the world had been affected by the virus.

Castro provided evidence that the use of biological weapons against Cuba had been long contemplated by the CIA, a subject even discussed at U.S. Congressional hearings in 1969, and referred to in the 1975 U.S. Senate Select Committee investigating the activities of the CIA.

Approximately at the same time that Castro's address was being delivered, independent corroborating evidence of his charge appeared in a book *The Fish is Red—The Story of the Secret War Against Cuba,* written by Warren Hinckle and William Turner (Harper and Row, New York, 1981). Turner had been a CIA agent for ten years and the book's title comes from a phrase "The sky is blue . . . the fish is red," contained in a CIA coded message sent to Cuba at the time of the Bay of Pigs invasion.

The first use of both biological and weather warfare against Cuba, according to Hinckle and Turner, took place in 1969 when Richard Nixon was President:

> In March 1970 a U.S. intelligence officer passed a viral of African swine virus to a terrorist group. . . . Six weeks later Cuba suffered the first outbreak of swine fever in the Western Hemisphere; pig herds were decimated, causing a serious shortage of pork, the nation's dietary staple. The United Nation's Food and Agricultural Organization called

it the "most alarming" event of the year and futilely tried to track down "how the disease had been transmitted".

Also:

During 1969 and 1970 the CIA deployed futuristic weather modification technology to ravage Cuba's sugar crop and undermine the economy. Planes from the China Lake Naval Center in the California desert, where hi-tech was developed, overflew the island, seeding rain clouds with crystals that precipitated torrential rains over nonagricultural areas and left the cane fields arid (the downpours caused killer flash floods in some areas) [p. 293].

There is thus substantial evidence that the CIA has engaged in biological and weather warfare against the Cuban people.

The Fish Is Red also throws indirect light on the probable reason for Reagan's pardon of Eugenio Martínez, the only convicted Watergate burglar to be pardoned. Reagan said at the time (early 1983), that Martínez was not a ringleader in the Watergate crime and had lived up to the letter of the law since his release from prison. Former CIA director Richard Helms had likewise downplayed Martínez's role when he testified before the Watergate Committee. He treated Martínez as just a small fish caught in the Watergate net, without telling the committee anything about Martínez's real background.

Hinckle and Turner, however, provide evidence that Martínez was the most experienced and effective CIA operative "who guided the clandestine inshore runs to Cuba, to land agents or to pick them up." On one of these runs, in December 1961, a railroad bridge was blown up and a sugar warehouse set on fire. "I have personally carried out over 350 missions to Cuba for the CIA," Martínez boasted.

As Reagan knew of Martínez's long record of terrorist raids on Cuba, Reagan and the CIA must have something in mind that requires the professional services of their ace dynamite-runner.

WHAT ARE THE REASONS given for this "anything goes" type of warfare against the Cuban people? Reagan speaks a great deal about human rights, yet his administration, even more than those before him, has given huge amounts of military and economic aid to the most depraved and brutal regimes in our hemisphere and the world. Castro has said that the test of human rights is the economic blockade: "How can any government that maintains a criminal blockade, that attempts to starve millions of human beings, speak of human rights?"

This raises an aspect of human rights conveniently overlooked by those who speak of them the most. They never seem to consider employment, decent housing, educational opportunities, free medical care and racial equality in the category of human rights. That is why the U.S. delegation to the U.N., headed by Jeanne Kirkpatrick, had a sole vote cast against authorizing a study on "the right of adequate food as a human right." The U.S. representative said it was "questionable that the right to food was a *human* right"(!) which, of course, explains a great deal about U.S. foreign policy.

Much has also been said about Cuban "political prisoners." But if the U.S. stopped sending terrorist dynamiting agents into Cuba, such as those that Eugenio Martínez led, there would be fewer counterrevolutionaries to be caught and imprisoned. On this matter Castro has said, "After all the crimes the U.S. has committed against our country, it has no moral basis to look our country in the face."

Cuba is also charged with transshipping arms received from the Soviet Union to revolutionary forces in other Latin American countries. While asserting Cuba's right to give aid to others, Castro has repeatedly said that the written agreements between Cuba and the Soviet Union strictly stipulate that Soviet arms cannot be sent to any other country and that their sole purpose is for Cuban domestic defense. The Cubans insist that they have never violated this agreement.

In regard to Cuban military aid to Angola and other African states, Castro asserts the right to help such friendly nations. "We're supporting African governments that have requested our cooperation; they are duly constituted governments, and revolutionary and progressive governments. Our military advisers are not lending their services to any fascist government anywhere in the world, or to any reactionary governments." Fidel contrasts this with the constant aid being given by the U.S. to the racist, apartheid government of South Africa.

Castro challenges the moral right of the U.S. Government to speak about Cuban troops in Africa, when it has more than 350 military bases around the world and hundreds of thousands of U.S. soldiers on foreign soil. "What moral right does the U.S. have to use the argument of our troops being in Africa when its own troops are stationed here in our national territory, at Guantánamo Naval Base? It we're going to talk about troops stationed where they shouldn't be, and that indeed has a lot to do with the bilateral relations between Cuba and the U.S., the only troops that should be talked about are those at the Guantánamo Naval Base."

It would be ridiculous, Castro has said, if Cuba were to demand that the U.S. first withdraw its troops from the Philippines, or Turkey, or elsewhere, before being ready to discuss bilateral relations with it. "If we said that to the U.S., it would say, 'Those guys are crazy.' Therefore, how do they have the right to say it to us? Because they don't start with a logical premise, that of equality. It's 'all right' for the imperialists to have troops and advisers everywhere in the world, but we can't have them anywhere."

In his speech in Miami, Reagan accused Cuba of sending young people to serve in Africa against their will. The simple fact is that only volunteers are sent on such missions and that those who apply outnumber those who are selected by a ratio of ten to one.

The U.S. has accused Cuba of being a surrogate of the Soviet Union, actually a pawn doing its bidding in Africa and elsewhere. That this insult can be made against Cuba and its leaders is but another example of the arrogance of U.S. rulers, for whom a small nation has no right to independence and, in fact, cannot be independent.

Cuba's close economic ties with the Soviet Union are offered as evidence of its subservience. But Cuba did not break the sugar pact with the U.S. or impose an economic blockade against it. Our government did these vile deeds to Cuba. If they did not succeed in starving Cuba into submission, thanks are due to the Soviet Union and other socialist states that bought the sugar so arrogantly and arbitrarily rejected by the U.S., and under conditions of equality and mutual benefit.

No wonder Castro has said that if Washington expects Cuba to break its relations with the Soviet Union as prior condition for U.S. recognition, Cuba will just have to live without it.

ESTABLISHING NORMAL DIPLOMATIC and trade relations with

Cuba is too important to be left solely to the judgment of Washington administrations. The people of the U.S. have a stake in the outcome. Relations with Cuba are in many ways a barometer of how we relate to all the peoples of Latin America and the "Third World," and to the socialist lands as well. It could point either to fair weather or foul weather—to peace or war.

Learning to live with the new Cuba should not depend upon whether our government likes or dislikes her form of government and social system. All it requires is that we recognize Cuba's prerogative to exercise the rights proclaimed in our own revolutionary Declaration of Independence—"to institute new Government, laying its Foundation on such Principles and organizing its Powers in such Form, as to them shall seem most likely to effect their safety and happiness."

Other books by Gil Green

What's Happening to Labor (1976)
Portugal's Revolution (1976)
The New Radicalism (1971)
Revolution Cuban Style (1970)
The Enemy Forgotten (1956)